THE SWISS ARMY KNIFE 63 BOOK

OUTDOOR PROJECTS

FELIX IMMLER

PHOTOGRAPHY BY
MATTHEW WORDEN

THE SWISS ARMY KNIFE

63 BOOK

OUTDOOR PROJECTS

FRANCES LINCOLN

Shelving 64

Wash station 90

Table made of branches 82

Cooking utensils 106

Improvised tools and implements 14

Ladder 32

Leaf rake 34

Table 60

Stone tools 38

Seat cushion 102

Three-legged stool 88

Loom 102

Bench 62

Sloping roof 48

Clothes hanger 97

ushcraft chair 85

Stone oven 70

Broom 27

Pot holder 150

Light and heat
reflector 57

Bed 54

Fridge 67

Fireplace 57

CONTENTS

THE ESSENTIALS

FOREWORD

There are books, videos and workshops that will tell you how to survive extreme conditions in the Himalaya or the Sahara, or how to get through a disaster in a major city. Finding inspiration for exciting adventures in the woods is somewhat more difficult. Yet heading out into the forest with sufficient supplies in your backpack and camping out there is something that lots of nature-lovers do on a regular basis.

I hope to bridge the gap with this book, by showing just how much fun you can have by making everyday objects for yourself, using only natural materials and your pocket knife as tools, creating a comfortable camp in the wild and having a thrilling trip amid the great outdoors. While luxury is something that we take for granted within our own four walls, making it for yourself out in the open is ten times as much fun. You only truly appreciate a watertight roof, a fridge or a comfortable stool when you're in the middle of nowhere. And then you can also enjoy the unbeatable experience of whittling a spoon or fork for your forest picnic yourself.

As a nature instructor I'm particularly keen to pass on a love of living with and alongside nature to young people. Going 'back to nature' is something you hear a lot about, but it's more than a matter of simply roasting a sausage over an open fire. You need much more exciting tasks than that, or the PlayStation and other such attractions will invariably gain the upper hand. There are lots of exciting yet comfortable activities to be enjoyed at home, and these compete with the experiences that the outside world has to offer. This makes it all the more important for parents, educators, teachers, youth group leaders and other caregivers to have a stash of fascinating ideas in their arsenal. By gathering a wide range of project ideas together in this book, I also hope to appeal to hunters, rangers, walkers, camping enthusiasts, canoeists, mushroom pickers and all kinds of other nature-lovers who want to expand their outdoor repertoire.

There's no need for expensive outdoor equipment to do the projects in this book. A Swiss Army Knife with a wood saw will be quite sufficient to tackle many of these bushcraft ideas. Of course, having an axe, folding saw and a survival knife will hardly put you at a disadvantage. Personally, I enjoyed the challenge of doing these projects with as few shop-bought tools and implements as possible; after all, these additional tools aren't normally among the equipment carried by your average forest walker or hiker. If you're prepared to pare things back and have a few tricks up your sleeve, this pocket-sized workshop will provide everything you need to achieve your objective. You can find more information on how to use your pocket knife on page 192.

So what are you waiting for? Pack your knife and get outdoors!

Felix Immler

INTRODUCTION

What is bushcraft, exactly?

There's no set-in-stone definition of the term 'bushcraft'. Generally speaking, it is understood as knowledge, skills and handicraft techniques that make life outdoors and amid nature more comfortable. As such, the trappings of civilisation are avoided as much as possible, and natural materials and simple tools used in their place.

Unlike survival techniques, bushcraft is not about outright emergency situations in which it may be a case of life or death. As such, there's no need to agonise over the time and effort spent on every single action. Bushcrafters actively plan to spend time in the woods and set about making nature their refuge for the sheer joy of it. They don't start off by asking themselves how much time and energy it's going to take. In a survival situation, a person is likely to choose the shelter of a fir tree bristling with branches, rather than unnecessarily wasting energy on building a roof. In those circumstances, the aim is often to return from the wilderness to civilisation in one piece and as quickly as possible. By contrast, bushcrafters are looking to escape civilisation for a while and settle comfortably into nature. They will normally carry food, drinks and other essential equipment in their backpack. When compiling this book, I therefore deliberately omitted survival-specific topics such as trap-making, hunting, emergency foraging for edible plants and drinking water treatment.

The tools on the Swiss Army Knife that I use most for these projects are the saw, the blade and the reamer. Every Victorinox pocket knife that includes these tools is suitable for the projects in this book. You get all of these on the knife shown on the book cover – a Victorinox Camper (91 mm series). A larger Victorinox pocket knife from the 111 mm or the 130 mm series is an advantage because with the larger wood saw you can tackle branches as thick as an arm. The model I tend to use is the Victorinox Ranger Grip 79 (130 mm series). That is the one you see me using inside the book. I would recommend that younger readers use knives only with adult supervision. Make sure your knife stays in good condition: only a sharp knife is a safe knife!

The Ranger Grip knife I use in this book has a one hand locking blade. Laws in the UK and some US states require you to have a good reason to carry one, whether for work or any outdoor activity. Please inform yourself of local laws concerning one hand lockable knives before you use one or carry it on your person.

IMPROVISED TOOLS AND IMPLEMENTS

You won't necessarily need your
pocket knife for some projects. That said,
the improvised tools and implements
used for such projects – for instance, the
digging stick, wooden mallet and shovel
– have all been made using a method
in which the pocket knife is the only
shop-bought tool.

WOODEN MALLET

Anyone looking to set up a camp or fixed shelter in the forest is bound to find themselves in a situation where they will need a hammer or something that will function as one. A mallet is hugely useful for striking things, for instance hammering poles or tent pegs into the ground, driving a splitting wedge into a branch or using a digging stick to extract clay. Of course, you could simply use a sufficiently thick, sturdy piece of tree trunk or a branch in place of a mallet. However, a real mallet, with a handle and a head, can be gripped more easily, so if you're going to be using it regularly, it is preferable to a crude stick.

Cut a suitable piece of tree trunk out of a dead or fallen tree – look for a section that has a side branch coming out of it at right angles **1**, **2**. In order to ensure that the head of the hammer is bulky enough, the log should have a diameter of around 8 cm (3 in), while the side branch should have a diameter of at least 3 cm (1¼ in), so that the handle is hardy and robust. You can cut up the hitting surfaces a little using your pocket knife – this gives the mallet greater longevity, as it makes the edges more resilient. This mallet is an indispensable part of any outdoor workshop **3**.

DIGGING STICK

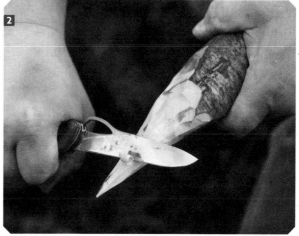

A digging stick can be put to a lot of different uses. It comes in very useful if you need to dig hollows in the ground, for instance for a fridge **1**, a toilet, gutters alongside your sleeping place or a fireplace. It is also ideal for making holes to anchor posts and supports in the ground. It is good for digging up spruce roots, which can be used as a binding material, or for prising large stones free from the bed of a stream in order to use them for your fireplace or stone oven. If you're on a steep slope, you can use your digging stick to cleave pieces of clay from the escarpment; these can be used to make a heat reflector or a stone oven.

To make a digging stick, find a branch with a diameter of at least 3 cm (1¼ in) and sharpen one end of it **2**. The length of the digging stick depends on your own size; if it's about as long as your lower arm, you'll find it perfect for most tasks. A digging stick can be made from a number of different kinds of wood. The harder and sturdier the type of wood, the better and more resilient your tool will be. In practice, however, you will have to do what you can with the wood that you find around you.

SHOVEL

It goes without saying that making a fully fledged shovel out of natural materials isn't possible unless you have a metal plate. However, a makeshift version that you can use to separate clay or scrape loosened earth out of a hole can still prove an efficient and valuable tool. Digging a hole by hand only works if the soil is loose beneath the surface, and you also run the risk of hurting yourself on sharp stones or other objects in the earth.

Look for a curved piece of branch or root **1**. Stretch this piece of wood to the length that you need **2**, and then cut the front section of the shovel so that it is fairly flat **3**, and then whittle the handle as necessary. Now you have your very own natural shovel **4**! A flat fragment or sturdy split-off piece of wood also makes a good stand-in for a shovel.

PICKAXE

An improvised pickaxe can also come in very useful. Of course, a wooden pickaxe is never going to be very effective in tackling hard subsoil, but if you need to dig a hollow in the forest floor for a fridge, it will prove very handy indeed **1**.

The basic material for this pickaxe was cut from a hazel bush that seemed to have been overturned by a minor landslide some time ago, pressing it towards the ground. The stems were almost horizontal to the floor. A number of sturdy side branches sprouted from the trunk, reaching towards the sunlight. These branches grew almost vertically upwards. If you find this kind of wood, you only need to whittle one end a little so that it is shaped like a wedge **2**, **3**. There's no need to do this to exact specifications, as in practice you will have to make do with the things that you find around you. Of course, you're bound to find other things that will work as a pickaxe. Branches that have broken off at their base, for instance, and taken a piece of wood from the trunk with them, can often be used as pickaxes right away **4**.

WOOD SPLITTER

If you need to split a branch, a fixed outdoor knife has obvious advantages over a folding or pocket knife. Personally, I only use my pocket knife to split pieces of wood with a diameter of up to 2.5 cm (1 in) – see page 198 for splitting techniques using your pocket knife. Pieces with a larger diameter require greater force to split, and there is just too great a risk of damaging the folding or locking mechanism – the Achilles heel of any folding blade – by exerting this kind of pressure on it. If your piece is larger than 2.5 cm (1 in) in diameter, I recommend only driving the blade into the wood until it is down to its back edge, and then inserting a wooden wedge into the split that you have made. Driving this wedge into the gap will split the wood. See below for how to make this kind of splitter out of wood using your pocket knife.

Making a wood splitter

Smaller wood splitters can be cut directly out of whole branches **1**. However, you will have to put a lot of effort into cutting it down until you have a flat, tapering wedge. The flatter the wedge is, the better it will be at splitting wood.

You can always find splintered pieces of wood that are almost in the form of a wedge already if you look around the forest – search in woodpiles or broken trunks and branches. Often you just need to make a few little adjustments with your saw or blade to get a very workable splitting wedge.

A small, relatively shallow wedge can also be made by splitting a piece of wood using your pocket knife. When splitting the wood, if you place your blade a little bit out from the centre line of the branch **2**, the wood will always split outwards **3**. This automatically creates pieces in the wedge shape that you need **4**. You can whittle down the bark side of the wedge to make it even flatter **5**. The tip of the wedge must be thin enough for you to drive it into a narrow slit **6**.

Wooden wedges cannot be driven straight into a piece of wood. If there isn't already a crack in the wood, you will have to start off by making a small crevice using the blade of your pocket knife. To do this, place the front edge of the blade at right angles to the piece of wood and carefully beat the back edge of the blade, using another piece of wood as a club, until the whole blade has sunk into the wood **7**.

Once you have carefully pulled the blade out of the wood, you will be left with a narrow crevice, into which you can then place the wooden wedge or wedges **8**. If the wedge is too short to split a stick, you can use the central section of the branch from which the wedge was split as an extension **9**.

If your wood splitter has a sturdier end, you could widen the narrow gap a little using the saw attachment on your pocket knife. Several small wedges can be used to make a larger wooden wedge using the same splitting technique; even logs of up to 10 cm (5 in) diameter can be split in this way (see page 111 for instructions on how to make a ladle).

BROOM

A broom is a useful cleaning device that has been used to sweep courtyards, gardens, streets and stables since time immemorial. Today brooms come in lots of different forms, but lots of people still swear by the traditional besom broom. Sweeping the forest floor with it would be a somewhat pointless task, but brooms can be put to good use outdoors nonetheless. Crafting a good broom out of dried brushwood makes a great project with natural materials. When I set up a camp, I use a broom to sweep the area in front of the fireplace **1**.

The broom consists of two parts: the broomstick and the broom itself. You need sufficient brushwood in order to be able to bind the broom together **2**. Thin birch twigs that have been stripped of leaves tend to be preferred by those who are accustomed to making brooms, but you could also use other twigs if you wished.

Once you have gathered enough twigs, form the stripped brushwood into small bundles **3**. You should use a handful of brushwood for each bundle. Twist the twigs slightly, working from the thick ends down to the tips **4**. Twisting them like this makes the individual bundles a little more compact and ensures that they hold together better. Other bundles of brushwood are arranged around the first bundle until the broom is at the size that you want. Finally, the whole thing is bound together firmly with a few tautly wound pieces of twine **5**. To adjust the broom and trim the twigs to the right length, bind the broom together at both ends and chop off any twigs that poke out **6**. Here I have chosen a broom length of 50–60 cm (20–24 in) **7**.

Bind the bundles together with more pieces of twine, keeping everything as tight as possible so that they don't come loose again or escape altogether **8**. At the top, where the broomstick will be inserted, it should to be bound at least three times with strong twine. Best of all would be to use wire, but you're unlikely to have either wire or pliers to hand in the forest.

The broomstick consists of a sturdy hazel branch that has been sharpened at one end **9**. Insert the tip into the middle of the upper bound part of the broom and hit the end of the stick hard to drive it 20–25 cm (8–10 in) deep into the bound broom **10**, **11**. Your broom is finished!

HAND BRUSH

Hand brushes are used for cleaning tables and benches, or for clearing the stone slabs in your clay oven or fireplace.

You could use the left-over clippings from a broom to make your hand brush, or gather extra brushwood for this purpose. Take a bundle of birch brushwood – about enough for you to be able to encircle it with your thumb and index finger. Bind the brushwood tightly together temporarily, and then cut the brushwood to length at both ends, using the big blade of your pocket knife **1**. Insert a sharpened stick around 30 cm (12 in) long until it is halfway down the bundle **2** and bind it to the brushwood as tightly as you can **3**. Make sure that you use enough cord for the bindings to stay in place.

LADDER

When building a shelter or tapping resin, a ladder is exactly what you need. You can also use your ladder as a frame for transporting large pieces of tree bark.

The verticals sides of the ladder (rails) are made from stable and sturdy hazel trunks, sawn to a length of about 2.5 m (8 ft). Ideally, you should look for two rails that have a branch fork in the same place . This means that the first rung won't slip out of place and increases the stability of the whole design. Bind the two rails together about 30 cm (12 in) down from the top . You could use a parallel knot for this. Fix the ladder rungs to both sides of the stringers; the rungs should be at least 3.5 cm (1½ in) thick. A cross knot is ideal . This simple ladder will allow you to reach things that were previously out of your grasp in and around your camp.

LEAF RAKE

Leaves are crucial for all sorts of bushcraft and survival projects, especially for making insulation, padding or sealing in the roofs of shelters. In all of these cases, large quantities of leaves are required. It is therefore worth having a tool that allows you to rake up large quantities of leaves effectively. Your starting point for your leaf rake should be a branch fork with a stem that has a diameter of at least 2.5 cm (1 in) **1**. Two more branch forks can be added to this

2. These are trimmed off at about 25 cm (10 in) before the fork **3** and bound to the stem with two ties **4**. A branch is then placed in the branch forks as a cross strut, so that the prongs come alternately in front of and behind the crossbar **5**. The prongs are bound tightly to the one another at regular intervals along the length of the cross strut **6**. Finally, trim all of the prongs so that they are the same length **7**, and your rake will be ready to use.

CHARCOAL STICKS

People have drawn with charred wood since ancient times, as we know from countless cave drawings. Drawing large pictures on stone or wood with homemade charcoal sticks is a special experience for old and young alike.

To make charcoal sticks you need an airtight, sealable metal tin or jam jar and sand or clay. Ideally you should use 1–1.5 cm-thick (½ in), straight pieces of freshly cut wood. For my first attempts I always used willow or hazel, but other types of wood will work just as well for making charcoal sticks.

Just as you would if you were burning charcoal on your barbecue, the branches are heated without an air supply, so that the volatile parts of the wood burn. What is left is the charcoal.

You simply need an empty tin can without a lid **1**. Cut willow branches to the right length for them to fit into the tin **2**, **3**. Cover the sticks with sand and press the sand down gently **4**. Leave the tin in the fire for at least an hour. After the time is up, take out the tin **5** and let the sand cool off. Check whether the sticks are completely charred **6**. If they still have brown bits, they aren't charred enough, so cover the sticks up with sand again and put the tin back in the fire. If you're using a

jar with a lid, it will take only half an hour in the fire, because sand needs longer than air to heat up. Alternatively, the branches for charring could be packed around with clay, but when the clay breaks down there is the risk that the sticks will also break.

Charcoal sticks are also handy for sketching contours before carving something **7**. Now there's no excuse for you not to flaunt your artistic side in the great outdoors!

STONE AXE

Okay, I'll admit it: the stone axe that I made for this book is more of a plaything or prehistoric-inspired experiment than a practical forest tool. But if you have enough time and patience, you too could try to sharpen an axe head. The hours of work that go into grinding this piece are almost meditative, and you'll feel as though you might well have time-travelled back to the Stone Age.

For your basic material you simply need a stone, which should ideally already have the wedge shape that you're looking for from your axe head **1**. The stone should be naturally hard, all of one type of rock and fine-grained. If it makes a bright, glassy sound when you hit it against another stone, that's a good sign that it is hard enough. Another rule of thumb states that the darker the colour, the heavier and harder the stone. You grind it against a soft sandstone that breaks down into grains quickly – look for one that creates a lot of grinding residue **2**.

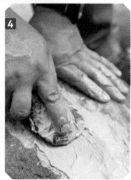

If you need to get rid of large uneven areas or corners, you'd be best advised to use the knapping technique. To do this, use another stone to strike at the areas that you want to split off from the rest **3**. With a little luck and effort, the stone will split just as you want it to. After you have roughly the shape you want, you will have to spend another few hours grinding your axe head until you have given it a workable wedge shape **4**. Aim for a convex, rounded edge when grinding the stone, as an edge that takes this shape is more stable than a flat surface **5**. To finish it off, you need a sturdy branch with a bend that is as close to a right angle as possible.

In the spot where you want the axe head to sit, use your wood saw to cut a notch **6** and then use your blade to split off the section of wood that isn't required **7**. This provides a suitable bed for the axe head **8**. If necessary, you can also whittle the shape of this seat a little more so that it fits the shape of the stone. Attach the axe head temporarily to the stick with twine and drip burning resin into the gap between the wood and stone **9**. Use lots of twine to bind the axe head, making sure that it is absolutely secure **10**, and rub these twine ties with resin, too. This holds the fibres together more strongly, while the additional frictional resistance prevents the twine from slipping and the axe head from coming loose, while also making it safer to use.

If you wish, you could now use the axe to chip off small side branches **11**.

STONE KNIFE

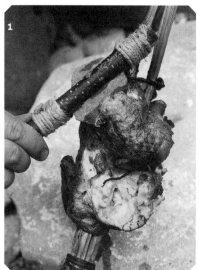

A stone knife made from an ordinary river stone is remarkably good at cutting meat **1**, vegetables and plant fibres. The blade is made from a simple stone chipping. So far I have had success with fine-grained, uniform river stones such as limestone, basalt and quartz. Sandstone, on the other hand, is not suitable. Discover for yourself which stones from your local area provide good chippings.

You should look for a flat stone with a protruding edge. Strike this edge hard with another fist-sized stone **2**, so that the jutting edge receives glancing blows. With a little luck, a chip will come off the underside, leaving a sharp edge **3**. This striking technique is used predominantly with flintstone and is called 'flint knapping'. (You can find out more about this fascinating technique by putting this term into a search engine – there are lots of interesting pieces about it on the internet.) You then attach the stone chip into a stick

of about 40 cm (16 in) long that has a split halfway through it **4**; if necessary, you can whittle the split surfaces of the wood with your knife so that they fit the shape of the stone a little better **5**, **6**. Use twine or bark to bind the split stick and the stone blade together at the top and bottom, so that it is firmly clamped and won't budge **7**, **8**.

STONE HAMMER

The history of stone tools is simply fascinating. The oldest known stone tools are over two million years old. Rough stone tools can be made with just a basic knowledge of the nature of different types of rock and a rudimentary understanding of the methods for handling them. You can make an improvised hammer from a hard, oblong stone. Of course, you could simply hold the stone in your hand, but a hammer with a handle is more ergonomic and effective. The following instructions set out one version of this tool.

A sturdy branch, about 50 cm (20 in) long and with a diameter of at least 2.5 cm (1 in), is ideal as a hammer handle. Use your pocket knife and splitting wedge to split the branch down about two thirds of its length (see page 198 for the splitting technique) **1**, **2**. Bind the branch several times around beneath the split **3** to prevent it from splitting further. Now look for an oblong stone with a flat side. This front surface will serve as the hitting side. If you find a stone with an indentation or bulge on one side, you can use this unevenness to make sure that the clamped stone does not slip down between the two halves of the handle. If necessary, you can use your pocket knife to mould the inside surfaces of the split so that they fit the contour of the stone better. Jam the stone between the two halves of the handle and bind it as tightly as possible above the stone **4**. This ensures that the stone remains in place even if massive pressure is exerted on it; it is also secured with a cross knot **5**. Your stone hammer is now ready to use **5**!

FIXED CAMP
STRUCTURES

SLOPING ROOF

The ability to build a shelter out in the wilderness, using only natural materials, is one of the most important skills for any serious bushcrafter. This shelter or refuge offers protection and safety and forms the central element to your forest camp. In its simplest incarnation, you could simply spread out a plastic or fabric tarpaulin, and there you have your roof. However, building a watertight roof without any manmade resources ranks alongside kindling a fire by rubbing sticks together as the ultimate test of bushcrafting skills.

There are different types and shapes of naturally made shelters. Closed and open shelters are fundamentally different.

Closed shelters tend to be based on A-frame structures, insulated and made watertight by a thick layer of leaves. The shelter shown here has been made as small as possible so that the body warmth of the person within in warms up the inside **1**, **2**, **3**, **4**.

If you are planning on spending a night outdoors and have the chance to make a fire, an open sloping roof with a bushcraft bed and a reflector behind the fireplace is a good option. This kind of lean-to shelter not only makes for a comfortable night's sleep, but also promises cosy hours around the fire, even if it's drizzling gently. The following instructions set out one possible way of constructing a lean-to shelter.

You should take particular care over choosing the location of your shelter, and indeed your camp. You will find some key suggestions for choosing a good spot on page 203. The configuration of trees in the chosen spot will determine which of the trunks are best for having the crossbeam for the lean-to roof fastened to them. In the interests of stability, it is best to choose a tree as the support for the crossbeam on at least one side. If there isn't a second tree at the right distance and in alignment with the first tree for fixing the crossbeam, you can secure the other end of the beam to a sturdy tripod or a log that has been embedded deep in the ground.

Ideally, the open front of the shelter should face away from the side that is likely to bear the brunt of any bad weather, so that you're not fully exposed to any wind or rain. Looking for sides of exposed trees and rocks with a thick covering of moss is a good indicator of the side that gets the prevailing weather; as trees and rocks get more moisture from the air on the side that is exposed to wind and rain, they will grow more moss and lichen on that side.

Choose an angle of between 45 and 60 degrees for your sloping roof. The steeper the angle of the roof, the better the rainwater will run off it and the less material is needed to make the roof rainproof. You can use a little trick to get a 60-degree angle: break a long, thin hazel branch into three pieces of equal length and then tie the ends together. This will give you an equilateral triangle with three angles of 60 degrees. A 60-degree sloping roof works particularly well with fir branches as a covering, as the fir branches can be hung across the cross braces and slot tightly into one another.

For the shelter shown here, we used a 60-degree angle for the roof, which was then covered with fir branches. During the construction it became apparent that there was far too little pine brushwood around to cover the whole roof. As a result, all suitable material that we could find around the place was pressed into service, especially leaves and pieces of bark. For roofs that are mainly covered with leaves it is better to choose a shallower angle of around 45–50 degrees. With a roof slope of 60 degrees **5**, you run the risk of the leaves sliding off. In our example, we had to make a wider base out of branches **6** to stop the greenery from slipping.

A sturdy log or a thick, straight branch will work as the crossbeam. In this case, making a large roof for a camp that is built to last, we used the 10 cm-thick (4 in) trunk of a dead tree **7**; cutting it to size with the saw attachment on my pocket knife was something of an ordeal **8**. The height of the beam is about 2.5 m (8½ ft), but a sloping roof can be much lower. Support the crossbeam with sturdy branch forks rammed into the ground to provide the right angle for the roof structure **9**, **10**.

Then secure the crossbeam to the three trunks. Twine can be made out of clematis **11**, **12**. Add additional supports, depending on the length and heaviness of the beam. In our example, we supported the middle of the beam with another vertical and two slanting forked branches **13**. Lengthwise supports, as straight as possible, are leant against the roof beams **13**.

If you're keen to construct a bed or a bench within the shelter, this is the best time to begin, before the roof-building goes any further. At this point it is easy to determine the exact position of a bed. What's more, the bedposts are far easier to ram into the ground before the roof, and the rest of the work on the bed will be more straightforward, too. You can find the exact method for making a bed on page 54.

Once you've finished the bed, you can continue making the roof structure by leaning more long supports against the roof beam **14**.

Clamp the long supports to the roof beam using another crosswise support, to prevent the supports from shifting sideways **15**. Then place another two crosswise supports at the top of the roof **16**, **17**. You can hang fir branches from these, forming the first layer of the roof. Look for fir branches that have already been cut down by the forestry service. Now the roof can be covered in fir branches, hanging them upside down from the crossbeams **18**. Work from bottom to top so that the branches and needles point downwards in the direction in which the rainwater will run, ensuring that water won't be able to run underneath the branches **19**, **20**. Once the roof is completely covered in fir branches,

plug any remaining gaps by simply stuffing more fir branches into the existing greenery.

If there's not enough pine brushwood available, you can use other material to seal your roof. Large fern fronds work well **21**: they can be crammed into the mesh of branches in bunches, upside down, row by row **22**. As the leaves that will form the next layer are likely to slip off due to the 60-degree angle, you have to create a foundation for them first out of dead wood that you find lying around. In this case, some branches were rammed vertically into the ground at the base of the roof and the resulting gap filled with branches **23**. You can cover the roof with a layer

of leaves, making it as thick as possible **24**, **25**. As the final step, almost as a kind of roof shingles to prevent the leaves from blowing away and in order to provide greater protection against the rain, you can cover the roof with pieces of bark, again working from bottom to top **26**, **27**, **28**. Make sure that the pieces of bark overlap in such a way that rainwater will run over the bark.

If you want to spend the night in your shelter, it is best to seal the side walls with fir branches too, in order to keep out at least some of the draught.

BED

A bed sheltered by a roof serves not only as a place to sleep, but also as a seat beside the fire and as a storage shelf. To make your bed a comfortable seat and ensure that you won't have to contend with cold rising up from the ground while you're trying to sleep, it is cushioned and insulated with a thick layer of fir branches and ferns. I use a special technique for the substructure of the bed to ensure that it won't sink further into the ground once weight is placed on it. This technique also works with branches that have a relatively small diameter.

To work out the exact position of the bed, place a couple of roof poles provisionally at the same angle as the sloping roof against the crossbeam. This allows you to work out the exact position of the bedposts against the roof. Remove these temporary roof poles in order to build the bed before finishing the roof.

Now you need sharpened bedposts with a diameter of at least 3 cm (1¼ in) . Drive two posts into the ground next to each other, about 5 cm (2 in) apart ,

and another two posts opposite them, at a distance that corresponds with the desired width of the bed. In this case, the branches that come between these posts are trimmed to 80 cm (2½ ft) . Once you have established the height that you want, (around 35 cm/14 in in this case), bind the pairs of posts together at the top . Depending on the length of the bed and the thickness of the lengthwise supports that you are using, you should create two or three such supports.

Now you can insert the long supports **5**. In order to ensure that the outer wooden lengths don't slip out, tie them tightly **6**. The other lengthwise supports are also attached with twine **7**. Now you can insulate the bed with fir branches **8**, **9**. To prevent the fir needles from prickling you, top these with a layer of ferns **10**. Now your bed is finished, and nothing stands in the way of a good night's sleep **11**.

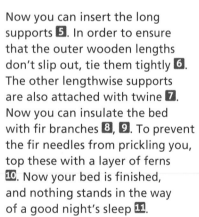

FIREPLACE WITH LIGHT
AND HEAT REFLECTOR

A few years ago I spent a weekend in late autumn camping with friends on a steep wooded site in the Swiss Alps, about 1,700 m (5,000 ft) above sea level. Due to the limited space and terrain, when building our fireplace we weren't able to maintain a sufficiently safe distance from a pine tree. We built our fire on a layer of clay and kept it small. The next day we decided to make a reflector out of branches and clay behind the fireplace, so that the trunk of the tree would be protected from heat radiation from the fire. Once we had done this, I realised just how great an impact this kind of light and heat reflector can have. Although

temperatures were hovering around freezing point, on the second evening we found ourselves sitting around the fire in our T-shirts. And the structure not only reflected heat, but also light.

When building a fireplace, you should bear the following points in mind. Cover the floor of the fireplace with clay or flat stones so that the fire doesn't make burn marks on the forest floor and to prevent any underground roots from catching fire **1**. Construct a border of stones around the fireplace **2**. This means that the

fireplace is set apart from the rest of the area, while light and heat are reflected and the surroundings are protected from flying sparks. A wall of dead wood is also built just behind the fireplace using the same stacking technique as for making a bed **3**, **4**, **5**, **6** (see page 54).

You can extract clods of clay from points in the ground using your wooden mallet and digging stick **7**, **8**. Knead the clay thoroughly on a flat rock and add a little water **9**. Using a swinging motion, slap balls of the clay against the wall of branches so that the clay gets pressed between them **10**, **11**, **12**. A layer of clay was also applied to the back wall of the reflector **13**. And now the wall is complete **14**. The drying of the clay can be sped up by lighting a small fire, and this will ensure that the heavy clay doesn't start slipping off the reflector wall **15**.

BOARD TABLE

A table at which you can eat and work, or simply as a place to store things, makes a very useful addition to your camp. You can also place a cup on a board table in the certainty that it won't topple over, or place a knife there, knowing that it won't fall onto the ground.

Your basic materials are four sturdy forked branches and two strong struts **1**. You can use a tool to make holes in the ground for the table legs **2**. If the subsoil is too rocky to make holes that are deep enough, you can use a special trick: to make the table legs more stable, drive three extra wedges into the ground **3** and lash these together with twine 15cm (6 in) above the ground **4**.

Then place the struts in the forks and fasten them with twine **5**. This provides a relatively stable framework upon which you can now lay the boards **6**, **7**. You can read more about finding, sourcing and cutting the boards to length on page 189.

BENCH

If you want to be able to sit comfortably at your table, you will need a bench. The bench is made using the same technique as for the bed – see page 54. You need four sharpened posts for each side of the bench, each at least 3 cm (1¼ in) in diameter. Two posts are beaten into the ground next to each other, about 5cm (2 in) apart. The branches that are slotted between these posts should be trimmed to 50 cm (20 in).

Once you have your sticks at the right height (in this case about 35 cm/14 in), bind the pairs of posts together at the upper end **1**, **2**. To make the seat surface use sturdy lengths of wood with a diameter of at least 4 cm (1½ in) **3**, **4**. In our example, the sturdiness of the branches used for the seat meant that we only needed the two supports at the ends; a third in the middle of the bench wasn't necessary.

SHELVING

If you've made a few tools and cooking utensils for your fixed camp, you'll need some covered shelving to keep your implements mostly dry and tidied away. To make this type of shelving, choose two trees standing close together as the side supports. This will ensure that you won't have any issues with the stability of the structure. Use two strong branches as the supports for the shelves. Whittle down the middle third of the supports or adapt them to the contours of the tree trunks so that they can be fastened more securely **1**. Attach the supports with strong twine, ensuring that they are as tightly bound to the tree trunks as possible **2**. In order to improve the strength of the bindings, it is worth making a couple of extra crosswise ties between each tree trunk and the support at the end **3**. Use two rods to measure the exact distance and apply this to the length of the first shelf **4**, **5**, **6**, **7**. You can find out how to make the boards for the shelves on page 189. Once you have done this, cut the boards for the shelves to length **8** and place them on the supports **9**.

If you have several narrow boards or only straight branches as your shelves, it is best to clamp the lengths of wood together and tie them at the sides in order to make sure that they won't slip off **10** .Once the planned number of shelves have been mounted **11**, you can proceed with the roof structure above them. Bind the roof supports to the trunks using the same technique as you did for the shelving **12**. These supports should be about one and a half times as long as the supports for the shelves. Additional cross braces are needed at the front and back in order to make a proper frame. Two forked branches are clamped between the front edge of the roof and the top shelf in order to provide additional support for the weight of the roof **13**. Now you can cover the roof with the materials that you find around you **14**. It's such a relief to bring a bit of order to camp life!

FRIDGE

If you're planning on staying out in the wild or in your camp for more than a couple of days, you'll inevitably be wondering how you can best keep your food cool until you need it. Meat and fish are particularly sensitive to high temperatures outdoors. Meanwhile, some drinks simply taste better if they're chilled. A friend once told me that on camping trips his father would always dig a burrow in the earth in order to keep food reasonably cool. I have used a burrow for my fridge, too. It also has a moist, breathable layer of moss, as its stored moisture evaporates during warm weather, sucking heat from the interior of the burrow. This trick provides an extra cooling effect.

You will need a shovel, pickaxe, digging stick and mallet to make the burrow **1**. First you dig a hole about as deep as your arm **2**, **3**, **4**, **5**, **6**. The one shown here is about 60 cm (2 ft) deep and has a diameter of about 40 cm (16 in). The edge of the burrow is made firmer with flat stones, as is its floor **7**.

Make two large grids of about 70 × 70 cm (2¼ x 2¼ ft) using interwoven branches **8**, **9**. To make a cover that will aid evaporation, follow these two key steps: first, place the first grid over the burrow **10** and cover it with twigs or fir branches so that it is even more finely woven **11**; and secondly add at least three layers of moss on top **12**, **13** before covering the whole thing with the second grid. Bind the two grids together with twine **14**, and your fridge is ready to use **15**. Even on days when it was over 30°C (86°F) in the sunshine, the burrow maintained a constant temperature of 12–14°C (53–57°F).

STONE OVEN

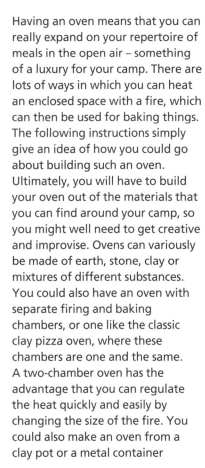

Having an oven means that you can really expand on your repertoire of meals in the open air – something of a luxury for your camp. There are lots of ways in which you can heat an enclosed space with a fire, which can then be used for baking things. The following instructions simply give an idea of how you could go about building such an oven. Ultimately, you will have to build your oven out of the materials that you can find around your camp, so you might well need to get creative and improvise. Ovens can variously be made of earth, stone, clay or mixtures of different substances. You could also have an oven with separate firing and baking chambers, or one like the classic clay pizza oven, where these chambers are one and the same. A two-chamber oven has the advantage that you can regulate the heat quickly and easily by changing the size of the fire. You could also make an oven from a clay pot or a metal container

embedded in the ground. Other options include a cooking pot with a lid or roasting things between two baking sheets. Here is one suggestion for how to make a two-chamber stone baking oven that is sealed with clay.

To carry the heavy rocks from the streambed to the camp, I made a hauling mechanism out of two small logs and a sturdy crossbeam **1**.

The first task was to make a solid base using the flat stone slabs **2**. It is best if the stone oven is set on a raised area or on a platform built specially for this purpose. Having the fire chamber raised a little means that you don't have to keep crouching down constantly to tend to the flames. The side walls of the fire chamber are made with large rectangular stones **3**. Of course, you could also use several layers of smaller stones to achieve the same effect. The largest flat stones that you can find should form the raised oven shelf **4**. The width of the firing and baking chamber is determined by the size of these stones for the shelf. The heat from the firing chamber rises between the cracks in the stone slabs and into the baking chamber **5**.

A second space, the baking chamber, is now built above the shelf **6**. You should also build a chimney in a suitable spot. To make the chimney, simply encase a stick in clay, and then pull the stick out once the clay is dry. For this oven I used flat stones for the chimney **7**, stuck together with lots of clay. Any cracks and gaps should now be sealed up with clay **8**. To enhance the look of the chimney, I also stacked up some stones around it, to make an attractive wall **9**. Now the oven is ready for its very first fire.

Do be careful: always begin with a small fire so that the oven warms up and dries out gradually. Also bear in mind that the stones may develop fissures or cracks due to the heat in the oven. You may even find that a stone suddenly bursts open with an explosion, sending hot stone chips into the air. As such, you should take care and be sure not to use sandstone or any damp rocks that have been lying in water when making your oven. Once the oven has been pre-heated until it is hot, you can slide your dish into the oven on a flat stone **10**. For this oven, which is made of thick slabs of stone, the stones took an hour to reach the necessary temperature for baking.

However, you can add your food to the oven much earlier if you wish, placed on a stone. As the heat that rises through the cracks only spreads out once it is in the chamber, we found that our food always had burnt patches if we put it directly onto the shelf to cook. It is also easier to shift the food around if it is on a stone. A board, baking sheet or flat stone would all work as the oven door **11**, **12**.

So now you can really get cooking! Your food will need more care and attention in a natural oven than it would in your cooker back at home. It should be turned regularly, as the heat is often unevenly distributed. That said, bread baked in this kind of oven is simply heavenly … if you ignore the charred bits, that is **13**, **14**!

My YouTube channel has videos on the theme of oven-building that you can use as an additional source of inspiration. See 'How to Build a Bushcraft Clay Oven' and 'Outdoor Pizza'.

HAMMOCK

There really is nothing better than relaxing in a hammock under a canopy of leaves, engrossed in a book or indulging in a nap. Well, there's no need to forsake this little luxury just because you haven't brought a hammock with you. To make your own hammock, it will be helpful to have a second person to assist you, as working with the long strands of clematis means that every pair of hands will come in very useful. When making your hammock, you should look for an appealing spot that has two suitable trees, 3 m (10 ft) apart. Two sturdy forked branches of about 70 cm (2½ ft) long are used to make two spacers **1**, **2**, **3**. These spaces will later be clamped between the outermost two skeins, thus tautening the hammock surface. You can find more information on gathering the clematis needed for the netting on page 186 **4**.

Backward-facing forked branches prevent the cords from slipping down the trunk **5**. The middle strand of the hammock is kept loose. Start with this strand. Take a 8–10 m (26–33 ft) strand of clematis and wrap it around both trees. Now wrap one end around the strand several times and twist the end, threading it between the individual strands. The strand is thus spliced (instead of just being wrapped) and will not come loose due to the clamping action or friction. Fasten the other end of the strand in the same way, ensuring that it sags slightly **6**.

The outermost strand of the hammock is now made, using the longest length of clematis. Wrap the strand around the two trees and weave the ends together. The spacers are used for the outermost strands **7**. For the remaining two strands, the clematis is simply wrapped around the two trees (without spacers) and intertwined **8**. Now weave thinner, bendier lengths of clematis at right angles to the long strands. This will take some time to complete, and you will need a large amount of clematis **9**, **10**. Lastly, use the remaining clematis to fasten the

spacers **11**. Your hand-woven hammock is now ready for hours of relaxation **12**, **13**.

You can watch a video of this project – 'Hammock Made Out of Natural Materials' – on my YouTube channel.

SAWHORSE

If you need to saw wood for burning or building things, a sawhorse will prove a massive help.

To make a sawhorse, get four sturdy branches, each about 1.2 m (4 ft) long, and sharpen them at one end . Drive the legs 20–30 cm (8–12 in) into the ground, at a steep angle . Bind both pairs of crossed legs together, about a quarter of the way down from the top , then fasten a long, sturdy strut of about 1 m (3½ ft) long to each side of the 'X', using strong twine . Drive two more support posts diagonally into the ground under the sawhorse so that their upper ends jut out from underneath the crossed legs. These diagonal struts should cross each other about a third of the way up from the ground . The support posts must be long enough for you to be able to drive them deep into the ground. Lastly, bind all of the crossing points tightly in order to make the structure as stable as possible. Your sawhorse is now ready to use. Using this contraption and the saw attachment on your pocket knife means that larger sticks can be made into firewood in a trice.

MOBILE CAMP EQUIPMENT

TABLE MADE OF BRANCHES

Whether you need a dining table, workbench, countertop or storage surface, a table top always comes in useful outdoors. By building a table you can keep important equipment off the ground and thus away from soil moisture and creepy-crawlies, and you can carry out tasks like preparing food at a comfortable height. Last but not least, eating at a table is simply more pleasant. And if you have two people to help with the carrying, this table can also be moved to a different spot within your camp.

Gather four straight, sturdy sticks about 2.5 m (8 ft) long, and 30–40 shorter straight sticks that all have around the same diameter . Start off by binding the long sticks together to make a stable four-legged structure ; this will form the basic structure for the table . Now tie two cross beams to the table legs, at the height that you want your table to be . Then place the other straight branches that you have gathered on top of the crossbeams, keeping them close together, to make the table top .

To give the whole structure extra stability, you could add another frame between the table top and the crossing point of the four-legged structure **6**, **7**. This frame can also be used as a clothes line for damp clothing or as a smoking rack for fish or meat **8**.

BUSHCRAFT CHAIR

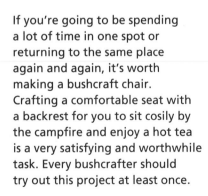

If you're going to be spending a lot of time in one spot or returning to the same place again and again, it's worth making a bushcraft chair. Crafting a comfortable seat with a backrest for you to sit cosily by the campfire and enjoy a hot tea is a very satisfying and worthwhile task. Every bushcrafter should try out this project at least once.

To make the chair, you need three strong, straight branches for the basic framework, two straight sticks as crossbeams and some smaller but still sturdy branches for the seat itself **1**. You can make this chair to different sizes, so there's no point in giving precise lengths here. That said, the branches for the basic framework should be no shorter than 1.5 m (5 ft). Ideally, the branches for the framework should be trimmed in such a way that two branches are forked at the level at which you wish to have your seat (about 30 cm/12 in up from the ground) **2**. (If you can't find any sticks with a branched fork in the right place, look on page 87 for an alternative solution.) Bind the forked sticks together at their upper end with a stick that is a little longer, which will form the spine for the three-legged structure **3**, and arrange the resulting tripod in such a way that the forks of the branches stick outwards **4**. If you don't have any twine to hand, read page 183 for more information about natural binding materials. Now place the crossbeam branches in the forks so that they protrude about 25–30 cm (10–14 in) on the seat side. At the bottom end, the sticks simply stand on the ground and are weighted down by a stone **5** or anchored to the ground with a sturdy forked branch, like a tent peg **6**. Now place the branches for the seat on the projecting crossbeams before securing the front branch with twine to stop it slipping.

The chair is now practically done. If you're looking for a bit more comfort, you could make a backrest by sticking another 4 or 5 long, flexible and somewhat thinner sticks vertically between the two branches of the seat that are furthest towards the back, and slot them into the forks of the three-legged structure at the top (see the image on page 85). The thin branches for the backrest will also need to be secured to the crossing point of the basic structure with a loop at the top.

Alternative versions
If you can't find branches for your three-legged structure that have forks in the right place for slotting in the bars for the seat, normal sticks can also be arranged into a three-legged frame, with separate forked branches tied to the front two sticks forming the structure **7**, **8**. If the sticks for the framework have a branch fork at the top, you can interlock them in such a way that they become wedged with one another and will hold together without the need for twine. However, to be on the safe side it is best to wrap them around a few times with twine or natural binding materials **9**.You could also use thin crossbeams as a backrest by binding them in the same way that you would for a rope ladder. The cross-branches are attached in such a way that the uppermost crossbeam acts as a large loop that can simply be hooked into the fork at the upper end of the basic framework **10**.

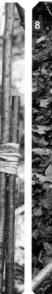

THREE-LEGGED STOOL

The three-legged stool is quick and easy to build. Remo, a friend and project partner at the Buchhorn Adventure Garden, showed me how to construct a quick three-legged stool using simple materials.

Saw three sturdy, straight branches with a diameter of at least 3 cm (1¼ in) to a length of about 50 cm (20 in) . Lay them on top of each other (two on the bottom, one on the top), and wrap a strong cord four times around the bundle, about a third of the way down from the top. Tie the ends of the cord together using a reef knot . Place the framework on the ground and spread the legs apart . You will notice the tautness that the knot gives the structure. Press the ends of the legs into the soil a little. You can now place either some horizontal branches , a small flat stone  or a large flat rock on top . And voilà – your three-legged stool is finished!

WASH STATION

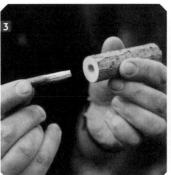

Hand hygiene is just as important out in the wild as it is at home, if not even more so. You just need a simple plastic bag and a few branches to make a practical hand-washing station, a convenience that is bound to go down well in any camp. Being able to stand and wash your hands or plates and dishes is much better than running the risks involved in trying to get them clean from steep, slippery banks of streams, where getting your shoes wet is the very least of your worries. Tie three sticks, each about 2 m (6½ ft) long, together to form a stable tripod structure **1**. In the example shown here, instead of tying the sticks, the washing station was made of three sticks with forked branches that dovetailed together in such a way that they were firmly wedged in position **2**. A short elder stick and a small twig whittled so that it tapered slightly to fit became the tap and the plug **3**, **4**. Use your pocket knife to cut a small corner from the bottom end of the plastic bag **5**, so that the elder pipe can be pushed through from the inside **6**. Seal up the passage with a few taut windings of string **7**. Now you just need to fill the plastic bag with water, hang it from one of the upper forks of the three-legged framework, and your wash station is finished **8**.

TIN CAN GRATER

The improvised grater shown here can be used to shred all sorts of food, such as cheese, carrots or onions. Here it is being used to prepare the ingredients for a natural chestnut soap.

You can find a number of natural materials that contain saponin in the forest, and these can be used to make a soap-like substance. Ivy or birch leaves are cut up into small pieces and placed in a container, such as a jam jar, with water. After a few hours of being immersed, the leaves release their saponin, creating a watery soap solution that you can use to wash your hands or clothing. In order to check whether the saponin has leached out from the leaves, shake the mixture a little or beat the water with a twig. If this creates a foam, then you will know that the saponin has been released.

Horse chestnuts contain quite a lot of saponin. I used to make soap by extracting the saponin from horse chestnuts as I've just described – by slicing them finely, immersing them in water and waiting for a few hours.

To make a tin can grater you need a tin with a diameter of at least 10 cm (4 in). The process is almost impossible with a smaller tin, as it will not offer enough room for you to get your hand inside it and use your pocket knife's piercing reamer. Push the piercing reamer attachment through the tin, from inside to outside **1**, **2**. This creates little hooks on the outer side of the tin that can be used as a grater **3**. Try to make as many holes as you can, spacing them in a staggered pattern **4**.

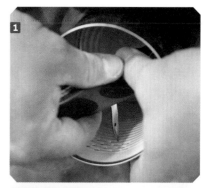

This technique requires very little effort. Be careful not to hurt yourself on the sharp edges of the hooks. If you want to grate horse chestnuts, you simply need to roughly remove their prickly shells **5**. This peel can be used as soap to wash your hands **6**, **7**, and seeing the soap foaming up as you wash them with a little water or grate the shell never fails to fascinate **8**, **9**. By peeling and rubbing the shell, this effect becomes even stronger, and this natural soap can be used to clean even the grubbiest of hands.

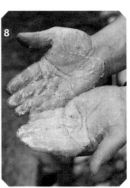

WARDROBE

You can tell an experienced bushcrafter by the way he or she won't place their backpack or jacket directly on the forest floor; at least, that's been my experience. Instead, seasoned forest hikers look for a tree trunk on which they can hang their equipment, keeping it off the ground. Besides ensuring that important equipment is protected from moisture from the earth, dirt and all manner of creepy-crawlies, this also means that your gear will remain dry and sheltered by the tree is there is a rainstorm. Look for some forked branches **1**. Level off the upper end of these forked branches using your knife, so that they resemble the tips of flathead screwdrivers **2**, **3**. Now use your reamer to make a hole in the flattened section **4**. Make this hole as big as possible. Thread the hook that you have now created onto some very strong twine – ideally this should be so thick that it only just fits through the holes **5**. If you only have thin twine to hand, as in the example shown here, I recommend using it to make a stronger cord. Tie the twine with a knot that is easy to undo – a reef knot is a good example – about 2 m (6½ ft) up a tree trunk. Now your wardrobe is ready **6**. By making sure that you can untie the knot, you will be able to take your wardrobe with you wherever you go.

CLOTHES HANGER

Although it might look like some sort of toy at first glance, if you're looking to dry or air clothing, you'll find this piece of equipment well and truly worthwhile. Clothes dry faster and are aired better if they can be hung up on a hanger when clean, allowing air to circulate between the front and back of a jacket or jumper. To start off with, you need a forked branch and a slightly bent branch, about 40 cm (16 in) long **1**. Cut a section out of the end of the forked branch to allow the two parts to connect **2**. Then carve a groove in the middle of the bent branch, to match the width of the flattened part of the forked branch **3**, **4**, **5**. Round out the ends of the hanger a little **6**. Now tie the two parts together **7**. Your outdoor clothes hanger is now ready to use **8**.

RESIN CANDLE

Warning: the resin candle should only be lit on a sufficiently large, fireproof base (for instance one made of clay, sand or a stone). If the bark's outer layer starts to melt off because burning resin is seeping over the edge, or if the resin candle tips over, the liquid resin can run out and start to burn. This can cause a small wildfire in no time at all. Never light your resin candle inside a building or somewhere with a risk of fire. Also note that resin candles can give off a lot of smoke.

Filling a flat-bottomed tin can with resin and setting it alight is a time-honoured way for scouts to make candles, but it is possible to make a resin candle entirely from natural forest materials.

To do this you will need a piece of birch bark of about 6 × 20 cm (2½ x 8 in). Of course, if you have a larger piece you can make a larger candle. However, if this is your first attempt, it is recommended that you stick with these dimensions. Together with the birch bark, you need a piece of branch sawn off to about 3 cm (1¼ in) long, which will serve as the bottom of your candle. This piece of branch should have a diameter of at least 3.5 cm (1½ in). in addition, you need a good quantity of soft resin and a few strips of willow or elm bark **1**. (See page 184 for instructions on making binding material out of tree bark.) Wrap the birch bark tightly about twice around the piece of branch forming the base and bind it together with one of the strips of bark using a strangle knot **2**. Now put the resin into the candle. Compress it firmly with a stick **3**. The edge of the birch bark should still protrude a little at the top once the candle has been filled with resin. Once the resin burns and becomes hot all the way through, it expands a little and begins to form bubbles. On no account should the burning resin be able to slop over the edge. Insert a narrow wick made of birch bark into the middle of the candle **4**. Wrap the candle around with willow or elm bark twice again at the very top and in the middle **5**. Be sure to use fresh bark for these bindings, because it is less likely to burn through quickly or catch fire itself.

When experimenting with this
project, I often found that the
liquid resin would run over the
edge of the candle – a drop of
burning resin would slop over the
edge, causing the birch bark to
burn from the outside. As such,
make sure that you pay heed to
the safety instructions in the box
opposite! If the candle is left
burning for a long time, a layer of
soot and ashes forms within the
liquid resin. If this is threatening
to stifle the flame, stir the resin
a little with a stick. The candle in
the picture burned for about an
hour **6**. In the interests of safety,
I would recommend lighting
several small candles rather than
one large one.

WOVEN SEAT CUSHION

If everything is damp or even soaking wet due to rain, fog or morning dew, you'll definitely appreciate the comfort of a seat cushion, as not only does it stop the seat of your trousers from getting damp, but also has an insulating effect that helps to keep the cold at bay.

Cut a couple of bundles of grass, as high as you can find it , . The perfect time to do this is on a warm and sunny morning. Spread these out on some short grass to dry . While the grass is drying, you can construct your weaving loom. To form the rear side, a horizontal cross-rod is fixed to two trees. To form the front side, hit four posts into the ground, about 50 cm (20 ft) from the rear side. These posts must be deep enough in the ground that they won't bend if the ropes are pulled. Four ropes of about 1.5 m (5 ft) each are knotted firmly onto the rear cross-beam, at 10 cm (4 in) intervals. Make the knots halfway along the ropes, so that that you have eight loose rope ends of about 75 cm (2½ ft) long.

Knot the pairs of cords that belong together twice again 2 cm (¾ in) down from the back cross-beam. Once the cushion has been woven, this will allow the cords between the cross-beam and the end knots to be separated with ease, without the lacing of the cushion coming undone **4**. Fix four of the loose ends of the rope pairs to the upright posts, ensuring that they are as taut as possible **5**. Place a second horizontal crossbar in front of the four posts, with the other four rope ends attached to this bar.

You should now take one bundle of grass **6**, lower the front crossbar to the ground and push the grass into the gap that has been created. Then raise the front crossbeam once more, cross over the cords once to the right and lower the horizontal beam again **7**. Now place another bundle of grass between the ropes **8**, raise the beam once again, cross the cords once more, this time to the left to return to your original position. Compress the webbing by pressing the bundles of grass against the back crossbar using your fingers and retighten the

cords a little **9**. The next bundle of grass can now be placed between the cords and woven into the pad. Repeat this process until the cushion has reached the dimensions that you need **10**, and then cut through the front cords **11** and tie them together **12**. Finally, cut through the cords between the back crossbar and the two knots **4**. Your grass cushion is now complete (see image, page 102). It also makes a very comfortable pillow for your head if you're lying in a hammock **13**.

COOKING UTENSILS

Be sure to use only non-toxic and tasteless types of wood for any cooking utensils that you make to help with cooking or eating. Suitable woods include sycamore, birch, ash, lime, hazel, alder and beech. Toxic woods (yew, robinia, laburnum, spindle and thuja) and woods with a high tannin content (oak and walnut) should not be used for cooking utensils.

TABLESPOON

Eating soup that you have cooked over the fire with a spoon that you have carved yourself is a fantastic, back-to-nature experience, and one that will both get your adrenaline racing and provide immense satisfaction.

Your spoon will be more ergonomic if the bowl (i.e. the concave dip in the spoon) is significantly deeper than the handle, so you should choose a dry piece of branch about 4 cm (1½ in) thick that has a slight bend in the middle **1**. Split the piece of wood down its length so that you have two pieces, each with a sharp bend. To protect your knife, insert it into the wood only down to the back edge of the blade **2**, then pull it out again and place a whittled wooden wedge into the split that you have made. You can then drive the wedge through the wood using a hammer crafted from a branch **3**, **4**, **5**. The outer part of the branch is used to make the spoon **6**. Using some tongs or two branches, take a piece of red-hot coal from the fire and place it exactly where you want the bowl of the spoon to be **7**, **8**. The bowl should lie just behind the bend and, once it has burnt out, have made enough room on both sides for you to grip the piece well for the final stages. Use the second piece of wood to clamp the embers carefully and blow on them with long, steady and even breaths **9**. You will be able to do this with greater precision if you have a blowpipe made of elder wood or Japanese knotweed. Once the workpiece is mostly dry, the embers will spread over the split surface quickly and begin to burn out the bowl.

If the embers are burning the bowl too much to one side or unevenly, you could spread a little damp clay around the edges, to prevent these areas from burning. One common error when whittling a spoon is to make the bowl too deep. This will make eating from it uncomfortable, as when you remove the spoon from your mouth, your upper lip won't reach the base.

Once the bowl is large enough, carefully scrape off the layer of coal using the rounded blade

of your can opener **10**. You can then carve the contours of the spoon around the bowl, starting with the handle **11**. Once the handle is finished **12**, the spoon is cut to length **13** and the outside curve of the bowl carved last of all.

In order to ensure that the wood does not break while you're carving the contours, keep a close eye on the direction in which you're cutting it **14**. If the wood fibres or growth rings become separated as you carve it, you will

have to cut from outside to inside – i.e. from thick to thin. If you cut against the outer contours, the outermost fibres and growth rings will no longer be supported by the subsequent layers of wood and can easily break off.

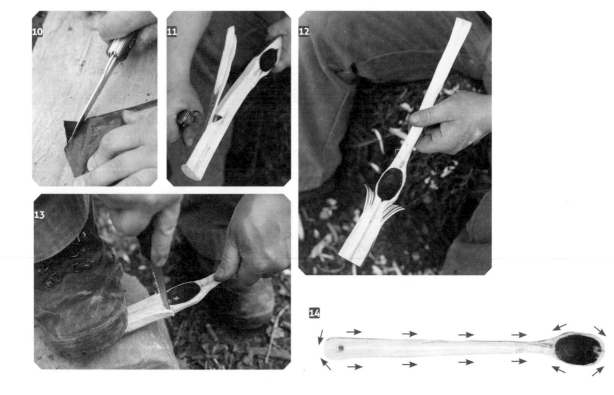

LADLE

We need a ladle to scoop runny or broth-like food out of a pot. You can make a ladle using your pocket knife and the burning out method that we employed for the tablespoon.

Look for a branch of non-toxic wood; it should be 6 cm (2½ in) thick at most and have a marked bend in it **1**. The drier the wood, the easier it is to burn out the bowl (the concave hollow in the ladle), but the harder it is to whittle the contours afterwards. Next, use your wood saw to shorten the branch to the length that you want **2**. Place your pocket knife right in the middle of the wood surface **3** and drive the blade of your knife into it using

powerful blows, until the back of the blade has gone down into the wood. Hit the middle of the back edge of the knife, holding the pocket knife loosely in your hand so that the force of the blows isn't transferred to the folding mechanism, damaging it in the process. Then pull the knife carefully out of the wood. The knife will have left a small groove in the wood. You can place a whittled splitting wedge into this groove (see page 24). If you wish, you could also widen the groove slightly using your saw **4**. This means that you won't need to make the end of the wedge completely sharp; instead it could have a 1–1.5 mm (¹⁄₁₆ in) wide strip, which will make it a lot more

stable. Now drive the wedge carefully into the wood **5**. You will see that the wedge tends to split the wood in line with the bend in the wood and the direction of the wood fibres **6**. If the wedge is driven so far into the wood that you can no longer see its long surface, you will have to use an extension and carry on until the piece is split **7**, **8**. Use wood tongs (see page 159) to remove a red-hot piece of coal from the fire and use the split-off opposite piece of wood to clamp it to the place where you want the bowl of the spoon to be **9**.

Blow on the coal with long, steady breaths of air. It will take a bit of perseverance before the embers

begin to spread to the wood, but when it happens it will take hold fairly quickly. By turning and moving the embers carefully you can change the shape of the burnt area **10**. You may need a new piece of coal every now and then. Before placing a new piece of coal onto the wood, scrape off the layer of coal that has been left on it using the rounded blade of your can opener **11**; this will allow you to get a better idea of where and how much you still need to burn away. If you have areas that no longer need to be burnt, spread them with a little clay **12**. A short blowpipe made from a hollow plant stem or elder wood will allow you to target air at the place that needs it more precisely.

Once the bowl is big enough you can carry on with the rest of the whittling and sawing **13**, **14**. When carving the outer shape of the ladle, keep a close eye on the direction of the wood fibres. If the fibres start to run crosswise or you need to cut deeper into the wood, you should always cut in the direction of the thinnest part of the piece, as this means that if the wood fibres start to run in a transverse direction, the wood won't break up. Now you can use the whole thing to ladle food **15**. Bon appétit!

BOWL

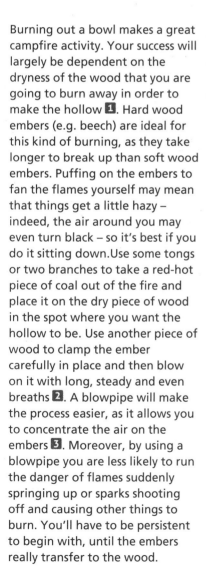

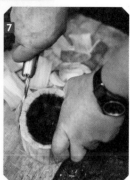

Burning out a bowl makes a great campfire activity. Your success will largely be dependent on the dryness of the wood that you are going to burn away in order to make the hollow **1**. Hard wood embers (e.g. beech) are ideal for this kind of burning, as they take longer to break up than soft wood embers. Puffing on the embers to fan the flames yourself may mean that things get a little hazy – indeed, the air around you may even turn black – so it's best if you do it sitting down.Use some tongs or two branches to take a red-hot piece of coal out of the fire and place it on the dry piece of wood in the spot where you want the hollow to be. Use another piece of wood to clamp the ember carefully in place and then blow on it with long, steady and even breaths **2**. A blowpipe will make the process easier, as it allows you to concentrate the air on the embers **3**. Moreover, by using a blowpipe you are less likely to run the danger of flames suddenly springing up or sparks shooting off and causing other things to burn. You'll have to be persistent to begin with, until the embers really transfer to the wood.

However, once this has happened, they take hold relatively quickly **4**. You can determine the shape of the area to be burned out by carefully turning and shifting the embers. You may need a new piece of coal every now and then. Before placing a new piece of coal in position, scrape out the residual layer of coal on the wood with the rounded blade of your can opener **5**. This will give you a better idea of where and how much you still have left to burn. If the embers begin to burn out the hollow too much to one side or in the wrong direction, spread some damp clay over the affected area **6**, as this will prevent any more of it from burning away. The burning can often cause small stress cracks, so it's important to make sure that the walls of the bowl are thick enough. Once the hollow is the right size, scrape as much of its

sooty layer away as you can. Lastly, you need to whittle the outside of the bowl to finish it off **7** – if you felt like it, you could even add some decorative carvings. Your bowl is now ready to hold a drink. Cheers! **8**

BARK SPOON

A bark spoon will provide a quick substitute for a spoon when you're out in the middle of nowhere. Bark spoons can be made from birch or cherry tree bark, which are leathery and can be folded without breaking. The bark of other trees can also be used – spruce bark is one example. As many camps won't have a birch or cherry tree in the immediate vicinity, it's worth experimenting with other types of bark that you can find around you.

Remove a piece of bark from the trunk of a fallen tree **1**, **2**. If the wood has already rotted, it should be very easy to strip off the bark. First, clean the inner side of the bark **3**, and then use a small forked branch to draw a circle **4**; in this case it has a diameter of about 10 cm. Make sure that your makeshift compass doesn't press a hole in the centre of the bark; instead, it should just leave a small indentation. Carefully cut out the circle **5** and remove the protruding skin on the outer side of the bark **6**.

Now make two cuts from the outer edge of the circle to the midpoint and place the folds that have been formed over each other **7**, **8**, **9**, **10**. This creates a concave hollow that serves as a bowl. Clamp the overlapping spot between a split stick, which will serve as the handle for the spoon **11**. This clamp can be made much stronger by winding it tightly with twine **12**, **13**. In this case, I used spruce roots in place of twine, but you could also use a different binding material or string. You will have no difficulty in making bark spoons bigger than the one shown here **14**. They are also ideal for ladling drinking water out of mountain streams.

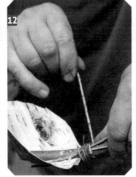

SPREADING KNIFE

If you have only one knife when you're out in the wild, you'll want to keep it safe and not use it for every single eventuality. You can use a suitable piece of wood to make a knife for spreading soft cheese or butter onto bread, for instance. Tasks that require gentle cutting, such as preparing vegetables or gathering plants, can also be done with this 'sharp' wooden knife.

With any luck, you'll find a snapped tree or board-like broken piece of wood that you can use as it is for your basic material. If not, use your pocket knife and a wooden wedge to cut a 6 mm-thick (¼ in) board out of a hardwood branch **1**, **2**, **3**, **4**. Use a charcoal stick (see page 36) or another drawing implement to draw the contours of your knife **5**, and then cut the knife out of the panel **6**, **7**.

In order to prevent the wood from splitting when you're carving out the contours, it's vital that you whittle it in the right direction. If the wooden fibres or growth rings become separated as you cut, you should work from outside to inside, i.e. from the thick areas to the thin areas. If you are cutting against the outer contours, the outermost fibres and growth rings will no longer be supported by the following layers of wood and can easily break free **8**.

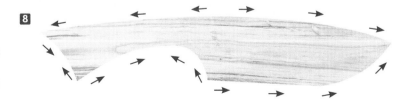

TABLE FORK

Whether you fancy some outdoor fondue in winter, tasty spaghetti with tomato sauce cooked over the fire or marshmallows roasted in the flames, eating with a fork that you have carved yourself is a very special experience.

In this case, I used a hazel root with a diameter of around 12–20 mm (½–¾ in) **1**. However, birch, maple, spruce, beech and other non-toxic forms of wood are also ideal. The length of your fork will depend on what you want to use it for. As such, a fork for fondue or roasting marshmallows will be longer than a normal fork for eating.

Use your blade to cut a branch into two pieces with opposing surfaces. The ends of the branch now look like large, flat screwdriver **2**, and you can cut prongs from this. If the wood is still 2–3 mm (⅛ in) thick at the end, use your reamer to bore a hole in the middle of the surface about (1½ in) from the end **3**. Do this with care – you don't want to split the wood. Place the surface of the fork on a wooden base. Put the top of your blade into the hole and work the cutting edge through the surface in such a way that you get a sharp prong **4**. Now press the blade through the wood using gentle seesawing movements. If you can't manage

to do this on your own, you could hit the back edge of the knife into the wood with a branch in order to push out the contours of the prongs. Finally, use your blade to whittle the resulting prongs a little more. If you wish, you can also whittle down the handle of the fork, too **5**. Now there's nothing stopping you from holding your own forest fondue party!

EGG BEATER OR WHISK

Admittedly, an egg beater or whisk isn't one of those absolutely essential utensils for cooking in the woods. However, it's nice to be able to make one out of the tip of a fir tree. And once you have one, you can put it to use!

Use your wood saw to cut through a trunk below a spot with multiple branches coming off it **1** – you're looking for a place with about 5–6 small branches. Now strip off the bark and any extraneous branches **2**. Cut the side branches to the right length for your whisk **3**. You don't need to find a freshly fallen fir, but the branches should still be bendable. Bend the first side branch towards the trunk and attach it with a few wrappings of twine **4**, and then repeat the process with the next side branch **5**. Carry on doing this until all of the branches have been bent and fixed in place. Bore a hole into the

end of the handle so that you can thread through a loop for hanging it up **6**. Your whisk is now finished and ready to use **7**.

If you shorten the side branches even more, you can make a whisk that can be used for tasks like beating cream **8**.

SPLIT WOODEN DRINKING CUP

Coopers create casks from individual planks using precise techniques. This split drinking cup owes something to this handicraft. If the wood has been split cleanly, with a bit of luck you should be able to bind the sections together to make a watertight vessel that can be used to carry liquids.

To make your drinking cup, use a piece of branch with a maximum diameter of 8 cm (3 in) and a height of around 15 cm (6 in). In this example, I've made a drinking cup from four segments. It is also possible to make a cup from six sections, which has the advantage of the walls being a little thinner. However, it does take more effort and it is more difficult to ensure that it's watertight. The basic way of making it remains the same.

Place your blade exactly down the middle of the cut surface of the wood **1** and carefully beat it in until the back edge of the blade is submerged in the wood. Pull the blade out of the wood, place it so that it is at a 90-degree angle to the other crack, and beat it once again into the core. Carefully remove the knife, and you will see that you now have two splits that make a cross exactly in the centre of the cut surface **2**. Now insert a wooden wedge into the splits and use it to split the branch into four sections of equal size **3**, **4**. Put the sections back together and mark which pieces go with which by drawing on what will later be the bottom of the cup with a charcoal stick (see page 36) or a pen **5**. This means that you will be able to put the pieces back

together later without having to waste time trying out different combinations **6**. On all four sides, saw a 2 cm (¾ in) groove above the bottom of the cup. When sawing, make sure that you leave at least 1 cm (¼ in) of the wall intact **7**. Split the inner part of the quarters off, so that when you put the individual pieces back together you have a cavity **8**, **9**. Carve out the inside walls of each of the four sides a little more; they should all be of the same thickness **10**. Now put the pieces back together **11** and fasten them around the outside with three taut bindings **12**, **13**. Weight down the cup with stones and leave it in water for a few hours, making sure that the whole cup is submerged. Once you fill it up, with any luck your cup should be watertight **14**.

You can see a video of this project under the title 'Bushcraft Cup' on my YouTube channel.

BARK CUP

This project caused me a few headaches. My first attempts at folding resulted in some leaky spots or tears in the bark. This may have been due to the fact that I didn't have any bark from a freshly felled tree to hand, but simply peeled some bark from a tree that had long been lying on the ground, whose wood was already starting to decay. It was easy enough to peel off the bark, but it had lost some of its elasticity. Only by leaving the bark in hot water for half an hour does it curl up and become suppler, so that it can be made into a watertight cup. The technique used to fold it is likely to be familiar to you from your schooldays – it is the same method as the one used to make a classic paper cup.

Cut a piece of birch bark from the trunk – ideally you should try to get as big and as square a piece as you can **1**. Clean the inside and outside by scraping it carefully with your blade **2**. Check that the piece doesn't have any holes or tears in it by holding it up against the sun or another source of bright light. Fold it once diagonally **3**. You now have a triangle; place it in front of you, with the top pointing away from you. Fold the lower right-hand corner up into the middle of the left-hand side of the triangle. This should mean that the upper edge of the folded corner is now parallel to the bottom edge **4**. Repeat this process on the left-hand side **5**. Fold the upper layer of the point downwards **6**. You can insert this tip by slotting it into the uppermost intermediate layer. Turn the bark over and fold the second point down **7**. Your cup is finished **8**.

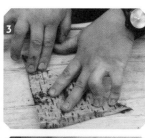

BARK CONTAINER

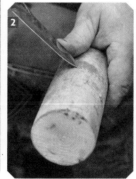

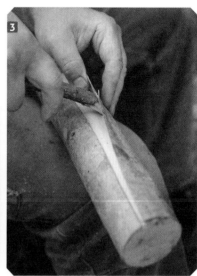

Making a container for gathering and storing forest materials can be invaluable when camping out in the wild. There are a number of ways to make such containers . The version set out here is a container that is simple and quick to make, but which is not watertight. Containers can be made from all sorts of tree bark, peeled straight off the tree trunk. In this case, I used a log from a freshly felled ash tree, with a diameter of around 6 cm (2½ in).

First, determine how high you want the walls of the container to be by tracing the blade of your pocket knife around the log, making the defining cut. Then make a lengthways cut. Make sure that these cuts are deep enough – they have to go right down to the wooden core, as otherwise the bark will not peel away easily. Using your knife carefully, now try to loosen the bark a little along the lengthways cut . If the bark lifts a little, try to loosen it a little more with your fingers or a sharpened twig, working with care . Look out for little twigs or other irregular bits of the bark structure, taking particular care that the bark does not tear around these areas. The piece of bark in the picture is about 20 × 50 cm (8 × 20 in). In the middle of the inner side of the bark use a blunt point to mark out the lance-shaped area that will become the bottom of the container .

Make sure that you don't cut through or perforate the bark when doing so. The shape should be very lightly carved so that the bark bends more easily around this shape. Now try to bend the container into the shape that you want. Once its side walls have been bent up, the lance-shaped bottom will take on a convex shape that gives the container remarkable stability. To sew the sides, overlap the walls slightly and then use your reamer to make a few holes **5**. It is easy to pull twine through the holes using the tweezer attachment on your pocket knife **6**, **7**. Sew the seams, making them as long and thorough as you can, provided that your hands can reach down into the container to do so. Finally, you can attach a length of twine to the top edge, allowing you to hang the container from a tree or around your neck. Now you're ready to go gathering all sorts of delicious forest treats **8**, **9**.

BASKET

Basket-weaving is an age-old technique for making containers for storage and transport, and is practised all over the world. Lots of materials are used for weaving, and there are myriad techniques for making baskets. I have set out a simple method here. It won't give you professional results, but will work for making many different baskets out of a range of materials. The essential requirement is that the materials used for weaving must be flexible enough. Anything that you can wrap around your wrist without it breaking is suitable for weaving; examples include willow, hazel, birch, fir roots, brambles and clematis. Willow saplings are the classic weaving material.

Gather a sufficient quantity of your chosen material – it should be as long as possible, and no thicker than 1 cm (¼ in). Remove any leaves and twigs coming off the sides. To make the basic framework for you to weave around, you need six 'stands' **1**. The twigs for the stands should be a little thicker than the rest of the material that you are going to use to weave your basket.

Make a 10 cm (4 in) slice lengthways down the middle of three of the stands **2**, **3**. Push the other three stands through the split lengths. This will give you a cross shape **4**. Insert two pieces of weaving willow into the split, thin side first, parallel to the slotted-in stands **5**. Lead one of the weaving pieces behind the stands and the other in front of them, then cross the weaving pieces and repeat, leading one weaving piece behind the stands and another in front of it. Repeat this process until you have woven all the way around the stands twice **6**. Now carry on doing this, but this time weave around each individual stand. In addition, bend each of the stands upward slightly before weaving around it **7**. After you have woven around each stand once, the cross will end up looking a bit like a wheel with spokes **8**.

Carry on weaving until you have used up all of your weaving pieces. At this point, insert a new piece behind the one that has just run out. Now continue with the new piece until you need to insert another **9**, **10**. Keep on weaving until the floor of your basket is big enough. The protruding ends are only cut off with a knife or saw once the base is complete **11**, **12**. When it is finished **13**, the stands can be sawn off **14**.

Select twelve side stakes. These will form the framework for the side walls. The stakes have to be a bit stronger than the pieces that are to be woven around them. Cut off the thicker end of the stakes at an angle so that you get a kind of point. Stick each of the stakes as deep as possible into the woven base, one beside each stand, sharp end first **15**. You will now have something that looks a bit like a sun with long rays. Use the reamer attachment on your pocket knife to make a hole in each of the stakes at the point where the side walls will end. Making this groove will prevent the stakes from breaking. Now place the whole structure on the ground and carefully bend each of the stakes upwards **16**. The stakes can now be bound together at the top **17**; you should bind them as close to the very end as possible.

Now insert two weaving pieces into the woven base **18** and weave the walls using the technique set out for the floor of the basket. The first few rounds are a bit laborious, as you will have to keep inserting the weaving pieces into the bound frame **19**. After four or five circuits **20** you will be able to cut off the top of the stakes **21**. Make the cut 50–60 cm (20–24 in) above where you want the upper edge of the basket to be **22**. Carry on weaving until your basket is the right height, and then weave the top edge using the remaining part of the stakes. Make a groove just above the last circuit of each stake to ensure that it does not break when you stop.

Now bend the first stake carefully and thread it behind the next stake **23**. Take this next stake, make another groove in it and thread it behind the next stake in turn. Carry on doing this until only one stake is left; thread this under the first stake and pull it through **24**. From above, the result will look like a sun with rays coming off it at angles **25**. Cut the protruding stakes to length, leaving about 10 cm (4 in) **26**. Make grooves in them using your reamer **27** so that the remaining lengths bend downwards and sideways at the groove **28**, and can be inserted below the next stake **29**. Your basket is now finished **30**.

HANGING BASKET

A hanging basket is the easiest sort of basket to make. All you need is a branch rosette from a fir tree and a few strands of willow or another material that is well suited to weaving. The rosette should have either seven or nine branches coming off it. If it has six or eight, you will have to weave two strands at the same time, as if you have an even number of 'stands', you will end up always weaving the same branch from the same side each time. For instructions on how to weave with two strands, see page 131 for a description of basket-weaving. If the rosette has an odd number of branches you will only have to use one strand. This will mean that after two circuits, a particular branch will have been woven around twice – once from the top and once from the bottom. If the branch rosette has only five branches, other stands can be inserted after the fourth round to the right and left.

This little fir sapling, which made a beautiful branch rosette, was felled during the thinning out of a young plantation , and the farmer let me have it after I asked. I shortened the branches using the saw attachment on my pocket knife . Willow strands left over from your basket-making can be woven around the branches, tier by tier , until the basket is big enough. The side branches are then trimmed once again and a hook cut into the upper end of the trunk section . This basket is ideal for storing fruit while you're in your camp.

CHOPPING BOARD

A clean and hygienic chopping board makes an important addition to your outdoor kitchen, as a place to cut up vegetables, meat, bread or cheese.

This wide, flat split-off piece of wood comes from the trunk of a broken fir tree **1**. A section of it was sawn off to make the chopping board **2**. Using a wooden wedge (see page 24 for instructions on how to make and use this), the bulges on the side are split off in order to make the board as flat as possible **3**. The rounded bits of the underside should ideally be flattened so that the board is even **4**, **5**.

ROLLING PIN

If you fancy making flatbreads and need to roll out the dough as thinly as possible on a flat stone, you will find a rolling pin a great help **1**, **2**, **3**. The example here was made from an ash branch with a diameter of roughly 6 cm (2½ in); in this case, it had already been peeled to make our bark container (see page 130) **4**. Now you simply need to cut the branch to length, and your rolling pin will be ready to use. If the branch has any bumps or bulges, these can easily be removed with your knife.

BRUSH

If you want to spread a chicken or a good piece of meat with marinade for a camp barbeque, you'll find that a brush comes in handy.

Cut a rectangular piece of wood from the trunk of a recently felled fir tree, including the outer layer **1**, **2**. Carefully remove the outer bark with your knife **3** so that you are left with the supple inner bark. Gently cut 2 cm (¾ in) deep into the inner bark **4**. Now make fine lengthways cuts as close together as possible to make the 'hairs' of the brush **5**, **6**. Clamp the brush hairs between a split hazel stick **7**, reinforcing the effect by tying them tightly together. Your brush is now ready.

POT DRAINER

This practical tool will mean no more burnt fingers and no more spaghetti falling splat onto the forest floor. Look for a forked branch – ideally one that is as symmetrical as possible. Cut both sides to length and saw a notch into the branch, onto which you can clip the pot handle. Find the exact position for the notch by measuring it against the cooking pot that you're using and marking the spot. When you drain off the cooking water, both sides of the forked branch allow you to tip up the side of the pot, making it all quite simple **1**, **2**, **3**.

COOKING AREA

POT HOLDERS

Height-adjustable pot holder with a swivel arm
(See image, opposite)

Before you can make a start on constructing this pot holder, you will need to beat a hole of at least 40 cm (15 in) deep into the ground using your digging stick (see page 18) and wooden mallet (see page 16) – this is for the vertical holding rod **1**. This vertical pole is subject to considerable lever forces, so it needs to be anchored deep in the ground **2**. It should have a diameter of at least 5 cm (2 in) and be as straight as possible. It is hammered into the hole that you have made **3** and then wedged in place with three large sticks **4**.

To make the horizontal swivel arm, you need a sturdy forked branch. Hold the forked branch against the vertical holding rod and align it so that the top fork runs horizontal **5**. Now you can make marks on the two forks and saw the branches so that they are roughly the right length **6**. The lower fork, which will bear the pressure, has to be split in line with the upper fork **7**, **8**.

Push a whittled wedge between the split surfaces of the lower support of the swivel arm in order to keep the split open. At its thick end, the wedge **9** should be as big as the diameter of the vertical holding rod. Fix the wedge in place by binding it tightly **10**. The rear end of the upper fork, which is subject to the tensile force, is then hung onto the vertical holding rod using another forked branch **11**. In order to ensure that the two branches do not come apart when they are under strain, you should cut sections out of them so that they interlock **12**. The joint is then fixed with two generous wrappings of twine **13**. The major difficulty here is in positioning the pieces in such a way that the swivel arm is ultimately horizontal or pointing slightly upwards. If you cannot manage to get it horizontal, it can be adjusted afterwards by moving the wedge in the lower fork of the swivel arm. To do this, you will first need to loosen the bindings, replacing them carefully again once you have made the adjustment. Finally, cut some more notches in the swivel arm so that the pot cannot slip off, even if it is being stirred vigorously **14**.

Pot holder made of forked branches with a crossbeam

To make this structure, you need two forked branches and a crossbeam.

By making hooks at different heights, you can raise or lower the pot over the fire **1**. This holder also allows you to have several pots over the fire at once.

To make a hook you will need a forked branch. Saw a cross into the branch at the end of the longer fork **2**, **3**. Cut out the section of the cross, leaving only the upper triangle **4**. Whittle down the inner part of the hook a little to form a grip for the pot handle **5**.

Pot holder: jib version 3
This popular version is the one to go for if you're looking to get your holder made in a hurry. You need a forked branch to support the jib, which will have the pot hanging at the end **1**. Use two tent pegs, which you can carve from forked branches **2**, or a heavy stone to secure the other end of the jib. To get an ideal distribution of forces, the back part of the carrying stick should be a little longer than the front, which will bear the weight of the pot **3**.

Pot holder: tripod version ❶
The tripod is the classic pot holder.
This height-adjustable structure
does, however, require rather a
lot of twine ❷, ❸. If the cords that
allow you to adjust the height are
simply slung over the tripod, then
the weight of a heavy, completely
suspended cooking pot on the
other end will create a lot of
frictional resistance. Ideally, the
twine enabling you to adjust
the height should instead form a
loop around the crossing point of
the three supports like a carabiner
❹, thus reducing attrition and
minimising the resistance due to
friction.

GRILLING GRATE

Camping in the great outdoors simply wouldn't be the same without succulent meat or other tasty treats grilled over the fire. This has long been one of the easiest and most traditional ways of cooking food outside. Thinly sliced meat can, of course, be cooked in the fire itself or on a hot stone, while vegetables can be packed in clay and baked in the flames. Nonetheless, grilled food remains the height of campfire indulgence.

Here are the instructions for a grill consisting of a sturdy frame, with grill bars that can be swapped out if they burn through. Both sides are supported by a stone border laid around the campfire.

Find four thick, straight branches for the frame and some thinner sticks for the grate **1**. In order to make the frame as sturdy as possible, you will need to use cross knots. On all four sticks that form the frame, saw a right-angled cross at the place that marks the extent of the grating **2**. The grooves should be sawn almost halfway into each branch. Now use the tip of your knife to prise out the two opposing triangles **3**, **4**. Slot the pieces of wood into one another **5**, squeeze them together and bind them in place **6**.

The interlocking triangles give a high degree of stability to the sides. If you wish, you can supplement this frame with a grid of thin branches **7**, **8**. Now there's nothing stopping you from holding your very own bushcraft barbecue! **9**

See the video 'Chestnuts Roasting on an Improvised Grill' on my YouTube channel for a look at this contraption in action.

GRILLING TONGS

Tongs are absolutely indispensable if you're cooking or grilling food over a fire, picking out pieces of coal, tending to the flames or gripping hot objects. There are different techniques for making them out of a branch, three of which are shown here.

Sawn tongs

The basic material for these tongs is a hazel branch about 3 cm (1¼ in) thick and around 80–100 cm (2½–3¼ ft) long. Halfway down the stick, carve a hollow about 20 cm (8 in) long, cutting about halfway through the wood **1**, **2**. Saw transverse grooves into this hollow, going about halfway through the remaining wood; they should be about 8 mm (¼ in) apart **3**. The branch is then bent around this hollow. Bend it slowly and carefully, providing as much support as you can for the thinnest area, in order to prevent too much strain or fractures at certain points **4**, **5**, **6**. After bending the branch, carve flat surfaces at each of the gripping ends **7**. You can also cut notches across the interior surfaces in order to make them even less prone to slipping **8**. Bind a length of twine around the hinge. These tongs can be made at any size **9**.

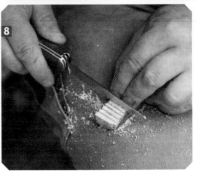

Split tongs

Take a straight stick of about 50 cm (20 in) long and with a diameter of 2–2.5 cm (¾–1 in) as your starting point **1**. Hazel wood tends to have strong spiral graining, meaning that the split surface becomes warped, making it unsuitable for making tongs. Ash, maple, lime or fir will be easier to split. Split the wood up to about halfway down the length **2**, **3** and then bind the branch just above the end of the split to ensure that it cannot split any further. Push a small branch **4** between the split surfaces in order to splay the arms of the tongs. Fix it in place with twine. Flatten the tips of the tongs a little more **5**. Now you're all set to start grasping things with your tongs **6**.

Broken tongs

Broken tongs are extremely easy to make and are ideal for fetching round objects like stones, eggs, potatoes or roasted apples out of the fire. As these tongs have a fork at the end of one of the branches, the object is held at three points of contact, clamping it in place more effectively.

You will need a branch of about 60–80 cm (24–30 in) long with a fork at one end. Mark the middle of the branch with a notch, which will also serve as a bending point **1**. Bend the branch at the marked point so that both sides remain attached **2**. The bent point acts like a hinge. Carve the side without the fork so that it is a little flatter. The tongs are now ready to use **3**.

BARBECUE FORK

The barbecue fork is a long-handled fork with at least two prongs. Unlike tongs, it skewers grilled food rather than clamping it in place. You can use your barbecue fork to turn large or heavy food on the grill or eat it straight from the fire.

Look for a forked branch with as small an angle as possible. Choose the sturdiness of the branch based on what you want to use it for. In most cases, the two prongs will need to be bent a little so that they run as close to parallel as possible. Wood bends more easily if it is heated **1**. If it is fixed in the bent position and then left to cool, it should ideally take on the shape that you want, but it will also have a slight tendency to jump back. As such, you should bind the prongs more closely together than apparently required for the end result that you want **2**. If you are using freshly cut wood, the forked branch can be heated directly over the fire. Very dry dead wood is best avoided as it won't bend. Damp dead wood should be immersed in water for a couple of hours first so that it gets completely soaked **3**.

Only then should you attempt to heat it, before carefully bending it and then binding it in place. After the wood has cooled off it is best to leave the bindings on for a few hours or days. Once the twine has been removed, the prongs can be whittled to the right shape **4**. Barbecue forks that have another fork towards the end of the handle make it easy to hang the tool from any nearby branch **5**. Enjoy your grilling session!

BARK POT

A few years ago a friend showed me how to make spruce needle tea in a handcrafted spruce bark cooking pot over the campfire. It was a brilliant outdoor experience, with a kind of cooking pot that still intrigues me to this day.

This project is easiest to do in spring and summer, when trees are in optimum condition and the bark of some varieties can be peeled off without any problem. Be on the lookout for freshly felled or fallen trees. Other trees besides spruce and ash are bound to have bark that can be removed easily for you to make your bark cooking pot.

Use your knife to mark out the piece of bark that you want to remove. Make sure that these cuts are deep enough, particularly if they run perpendicular to direction of the wood grain; otherwise you may find that the bark soon tears when you're trying to lift it. Begin by loosening the bark along the vertical cut, working carefully with your knife . Once the bark has been lifted about 1–2 cm (¼–¾ in) along the long edge, you can slide your fingers or a sharpened stick under the bark and carry on freeing it from the tree . If there are uneven or slightly damaged areas in the bark, you will have to be particularly gentle. Once you have prised away the piece of bark ,

bend all four sides upwards to form the side walls . The corners will form 'ears'; pinch them together, hold them against the walls of the container and secure them in place with clips **5**, **6**. These clips can be made of small hazel branches split up to three quarters of the way down their length. Bind them in place in order to ensure that they don't split any more. You shouldn't use your bark cooking pot over fierce flames; instead, it is best to wait until the flames go out and to hang the pot above the charcoal, or place it on a grilling plate on flat stones or damp sticks **7**.

If you place your bark pot directly onto the charcoal, the embers will go out under the pot because they will no longer be getting any air, so they cannot generate enough heat to bring the water to a boil.It is well worth trying out this rustic, traditional way of cooking.

A delicious tea brewed in your very own handcrafted bark pot is an unforgettable outdoor experience **8**.

BLOWPIPE

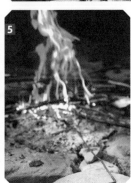

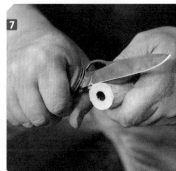

A blowpipe allows you to blow on a pocket of embers to rekindle a proper fire. The oxygen that is blown through it encourages the burning process and makes flames spring up from the embers once again. Of course, you can also blow directly on the fire with your mouth, but doing so will always mean a considerable risk of getting burnt due to the sheer heat near the fire. A blowpipe allows you to blow on the embers in comfort and from a safe distance, without ashes and sparks flying in all directions. The stream of air is concentrated and can be targeted at exactly the right place. In addition, it is more comfortable not to have to keep bending over the fire and getting your trousers dirty or your knees wet whenever you need to rouse the fire. A short blowpipe of just 20 cm (8 in) long, made from a hollow plant stem or a hollowed-out tube of elder wood is much more convenient than blowing straight onto the fire yourself.

Look for a straight length of elder wood, about 50 cm (20 in) long, and with a diameter of at least 8 mm (¼ in) across the inner wooden part **1**. If it has a side branch, you can use this as a grip or a hook for hanging it up. If you happen to have a piece of wire or a reinforcing rod, this can be bent and hammered into shape using stones **2**, **3**, **4** before being placed in the fire until the first 10 cm (4 in) are red hot **5**. The glowing tip can be used to burn out the inside of the elder wood branch. It works beautifully, but it does create a lot of smoke **6**. For shorter blowpipes, the inside can also be pushed out with a drill, a dried hardwood stick or a piece of wire. Whittle down the bark around the mouthpiece a little **7**, and your blowpipe is good to go!

BELLOWS

A large bin bag (garbage bag) can be put to fantastic use in a wide range of different situations: filled with leaves to form a sleeping bedroll, cut up to make a tarpaulin, worn as protection against wind or rain with holes for your head and arms, folded up to serve as a place to sit or insulation, as a way of carrying water, or inflated to make a swimming aid.

The sealing system used for Ortlieb panniers gave me the idea of using a rubbish bag as bellows, to provide a cushier alternative to blowing on the fire.

To make the bellows you need a bin bag with a drawstring tie, a couple of flat stones, two flexible hazel sticks and a pipe, which could be made of Japanese knotweed, Himalayan balsam, angelica, hogweed or a hollowed-out stick of elder wood **1**. Cut off a corner at the bottom of the bag **2**. Insert the pipe into the opening and bind twine around the hole until it is airtight **3**. The pipe is placed so that it reaches into the ember pockets in the fire. At the top edge of the rubbish bag, slide a hazel stick into one of the two drawstring openings **4**, then pierce it through the sealed side seam of the bag and back through to the opposite sealed seam. Do the same with the second hazel stick and the second opening.

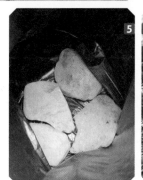

The hazel stick should be as long as the width of the bag. Place some flat, heavy stones in the rubbish bag to form a kind of floor, leaving the opening with the pipe free **5**. Fill the bag with air

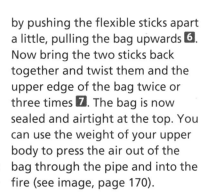

by pushing the flexible sticks apart a little, pulling the bag upwards **6**. Now bring the two sticks back together and twist them and the upper edge of the bag twice or three times **7**. The bag is now sealed and airtight at the top. You can use the weight of your upper body to press the air out of the bag through the pipe and into the fire (see image, page 170).

WATER-POWERED SPIT

To make a water wheel you need two forked branches as supports, a straight branch with a diameter of 2–3 cm (1 in) as the axis (e.g. hazel), six straight sticks as the spokes (e.g. hazel or dogwood), and six thin wooden boards.

The two forked branches are placed either on the bank or directly within the stream, which must be sufficiently deep and fast-flowing. If you're unable to plunge the branches deep enough into the streambed, layer stones around the bottom to keep them in place **1**.

Split the middle 25–30 cm (10–12 in) of the axis lengthways. To do this, place your blade against the middle of the stick and drive it into the wood, beating the back edge of the blade with a log **2** until the tip of the blade pokes through the other side. Then stand the axis up and expand the split by hitting the end of the blade carefully. While keeping the blade inside the split, carefully rotate it 90 degrees so that it stands up clamped between the surfaces of the split. Insert a stick into the resulting split **3**. Make a second and third split at a 60-degree angle to the first split in the same way **4**. The clamped stick

will act as a guide for you to get the splits at a 60-degree angle to one another. The spokes are now inserted into the three splits, placed around 20 cm apart **5**. Prior to slotting them into the split, shorten them to the right length. You can find this by placing the axis on the forked branches and measuring the distance from the axis to the water. To increase the effect of the clamped stick, lash the split axis between the spokes together with a length of twine. Use thin strips of wood – the kind that you find in snapped fir trees – to make six thin paddles, ideally of the same size **6**, **7**.

Use your large blade to split the spokes so that the paddles can be inserted and bound to them **8**, **9**, **10**. An initial test run in the stream will show you whether the water wheel is turning smoothly.

Now lengthen the axis with a piece of clematis. To ensure that the force is transferred, carve flat surfaces at the joins with the axis **11** and the length of clematis **12**, before placing one on top of the other and tying them together with twine.

The flexible middle part of the axis bridges the slope up to the grill. The other end of the length of clematis is attached to the chicken spit. The spit is split in the middle, with a small stick inserted into the gap to act as a spacer **13**. The chicken can then be placed onto the spit, and a crosswise stake skewered through the chicken and the split in the spit **14**. The water wheel can now be placed in the water. The chicken will turn a little erratically at first, as the water wheel needs to build up momentum that is then passed on to the axis. The different sides of the chicken are therefore exposed to the fire for different lengths of time and will have to be grilled a little longer at the end.

If there is no slope, the grill should work perfectly **15**.

Watch the video 'Bushcraft Grilled Chicken' on my YouTube channel to see the water-powered spit in action.

WOOD-FIRED GAS OVEN

If you compare just how much wood you need to burn on an open fire to bring half a litre (a pint) of water to the boil with how few wooden sticks **1** are required to boil the same amount of water using a wood-fired gas cooker, the self-made gas cooker is far and away the winner.

How it works 2: the wood-fired gas burner is filled with a handful of wood chips or tried twigs and the wood is lit. This initial combustion causes the wood to release wood gas. In a normal fire, most of this combustible wood gas would escape into the air without being used, as there is too little oxygen for all of it to burn. But in a wood-fired gas cooker cold air from the surrounding area is sucked in through the lower openings due to the rising hot air in the intervening space. The air that has been sucked in heats up between the walls of the can and streams through the upper row of holes and into the combustion chamber. This preheated air meets the rising wood gas. Now the mixture of gases contains enough oxygen for what is known as secondary combustion. This process ensures that the fuel burns more completely, with a hotter flame and substantially less smoke.

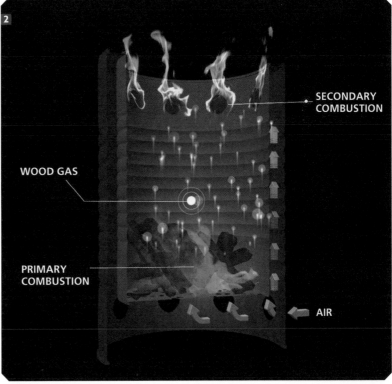

SECONDARY COMBUSTION

WOOD GAS

PRIMARY COMBUSTION

AIR

To make the cooker you need one medium-sized and one large tin can (diameters around 8 cm/3 in and 10 cm/4 in) **3**. For an effective windbreak that also serves as a pot ring, you will require another large can. However, there are other ways of making the pot ring and the windbreak – you could use bricks or clay, for instance.

Stand the smaller can on top of the base of the larger one. Try to place the small can in the very middle and use your reamer to trace its outline **4**. Now use your reamer to punch tightly spaced holes into the metal along the carved circular line so that you can prise out the circle at the end **5**, **6**. Punch two rows of 8 and 10 holes respectively with your reamer on the outside of the large can, near the bottom **7**. Perforate the base of the small can with at least 20 holes, again using your reamer. Bore another 8 to 10 holes at the top of the small can **8**. Now put the small can inside the large can, and your burner is finished **9**, **10**.

To make the windbreak/pot ring: you need another large can with a 10 cm (4 in) diameter for the windbreak. Work out which side of the can fits perfectly onto the outer edge of the burner (most cans can be stacked). Punch out the shape of the windbreak by making holes at small intervals, as shown **11**. Use your reamer to pierce around 30 holes in the windbreak. Don't forget to cut out the lid using your can opener before you completely detach the windbreak.

Your cooker is now ready to use **12**, **13**.

THE ESSENTIALS

Gathering bushcraft materials

You will need various materials found in the great outdoors for the projects in this book. As long as you're not in an extreme emergency situation, it's worth making the effort to gather materials from your natural surroundings in order to make the different structures and tools set out here, provided that you can do so without causing any damage to nature, or at least with as little an impact on it as possible. For instance, if you need a rainproof protective covering, you should use a thick layer of foliage or brushwood from a fallen fir tree instead of covering your roof with patches of moss torn up from the ground. Gathering moss leaves permanent scars in the moss carpet that covers the forest floor. As such, you should try to always use dead wood for all of your structures and projects. In addition, make sure that you don't take all of the plants of a particular species from the same place – always leave a couple of them where they are.

A reasoned approach and common sense should be the abiding principles of the responsible bushcrafter who is seeking to maintain a respectful relationship with nature. For more on this, read the tenets of the 'Leave no trace' philosophy on page 201.

Below you will find a few pointers on some of the natural materials that I tend to use for bushcrafting due to their specific characteristics.

Natural binding materials

If you don't have any twine to hand, then you could use natural materials instead. Admittedly, this usually means that you will have to spend significantly more time on the particular project, as such materials have to be gathered and prepared before you can use them. Some natural binding materials lose their flexibility when they dry out, making them more liable to tear. When binding things using natural materials, you are best advised to use knots that ensure that the binding strands change direction as few times as possible and that they undergo very little strain. I tend to use the timber hitch **1**, the clove hitch **2** and the strangle knot **3**, a knot that is very similar to the clove hitch, but which involves an additional lash.

What all of these knots have in common is that when they are tightened, they also become bound into place themselves. You can find out more on the internet, which has masses of information and details about how to make and use knots.

Elm or willow bark
In spring and summer, when the trees are in their prime, it is easy to detach elm and willow bark from freshly cut branches. As you peel off the bark it tends to become increasingly thinner, until it tears off altogether. Peeling the branch like a banana all the way around, pulling only a couple of centimetres at a time before moving on to the next strip, prevents the strips from tapering. This technique will give you long lengths of bark **1**. These strips can be used as binding materials as they are **2** or twisted to make a sturdier cord (see the box on page 187 for this twisting method for making a cord).

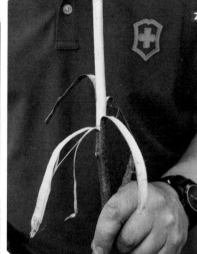

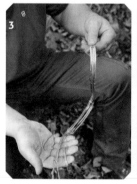

Stinging nettle fibres

Stinging nettle fibres **3** can be used to make very strong cords. To do this, you first have to separate the fibres from the woody part of the stem. To remove the leaves, strip the stalk from bottom to top **4**. An incision of a few centimetres (a couple of inches) is then cut into one side of the stem **5**. Open out the cut surfaces and, using the tip of your thumb, press down on the resulting slit. Split the stem along its whole length by running the tip of your thumb along it **6**. Now the woody inner part of the stem can be broken at short intervals and removed from the fibres **7**. To make a sturdy cord that will hold over time, the fibres have to be dried. Once they are dry, they can be twisted to form a cord **8**. (See the box on page 187 for the twisting method for making a cord.)

Grasses and rushes

Rushes **9** and grasses **10** can also be used as binding materials. While individual rushes or blades of grass break even when pulled gently, a thick strand of twisted grass or a bundle of rushes can withstand a large tensile force to a remarkable degree. Making this kind of cord is fairly time-consuming and will require a certain level of experience and dexterity. (See the box on page 187 for the twisting method for making a cord.)

Spruce roots

You can use a digging stick around spruce trees in order to dig up roots. Use your stick to scrape up the upper layer of earth about 1.5 m from the tree trunk until you come across a root strand **11**. Try to completely uncover the root, using your digging stick with care. If the forest floor is soft, you may well be able to carefully lift the root and thus pull it out of the ground **12**. These roots are very flexible **13** and can withstand considerable tensile force **14**. If you split the roots along their length and then twist them around one another, you will have a binding material that is even stronger and more flexible than its original form.

Clematis

Clematis vitalba, also known as old man's beard and traveller's joy, is a vine-like climbing plant that loves to climb up trees, covering them with its tendrils. As a child, I used to swing through the air on it like Tarzan, holding onto the hanging strands. The tough yet flexible clematis shoots have to be pulled down when bushes and trees are trimmed **1**, **2**. Doing this will often require all of your bodily strength, but they have the great advantage of being ready to use straight away as a binding material **3**. In my camp, I made the hammock (page 74) out of strands of clematis. If the strands of clematis are too short for your particular project, two strands can be spliced together by interweaving the ends of both strands with one another. From winter through to spring, clematis can be distinguished by its white, fluffy and round clusters of fruits **4**.

Twisting plant fibres, grasses and strands of bark to make a cord

Essentially, all plant fibres that are over 20 cm (8 in) long can be twisted to make a cord. In this example, I used rushes. Half of the rushes are placed over the other half so that their tips are at right angles to one another . Now hold the bundle of fibres slightly off-centre and twist them in upon themselves  until the twisted strand folds over upon itself, forming a loop. Grasp this loop with the thumb and index finger of your left hand. It is vital that the bundle contains different lengths, so that adding new fibres – which mean potential weak points in the cord – won't occur in exactly the same place in both parts of the strand.

Now take the longer bundle of rushes (coloured purple in the picture) between the thumb and finger of your right hand and turn the strand once in a clockwise direction . This is now brought around under the shorter strand, in an anti-clockwise direction . Repeat this with the thumb and index finger of your left hand so that the twisted strand does not unwind. Using your right hand, now grasp the shorter strand, twist it in a clockwise direction once again  and then place it behind the longer strand, again moving an anti-clockwise direction .

Repeat this with the thumb and index finger of your left hand so that the twisted strand doesn't become unwound. Repeat these steps until the shorter bundle of fibres is almost completely wound up. Then simply insert a new bundle of fibres and carry on with the twisting technique. This will give you a long and sturdy cord **7**.

Twisted hazel, willow or birch twigs

By twisting hazel twigs, like other fresh twigs, down their length, they can be split into fibres, making them more flexible. To do this, clamp the end of a twig between the sole of your shoe and a fixed object like a stone **1** and twist the twig in one direction until it begins to curl up **2**.

Now repeat the procedure, clamping the strand in place about 30 cm (12 in) further up and twisting it once again until it splits along its length and curls up once again. Repeat this process until the twig is flexible along the whole length that you need. A cord produced in this way will be able to withstand considerable tensile force **3**.

Brambles

Bramble stems can also be made into sturdy cords. Of course, you'll need to get rid of the prickles first in order to ensure that you won't get scratched. The easiest way of doing this is to rub all sides of the brambles over the edge of a stone, which will remove the prickles fairly efficiently. Now soften up the brambles by beating them with a cudgel or stone.

Branches and boards

Sawing branches off living trees is expressly forbidden, which means that we have no choice but to work with dead wood. I was lucky that about 250 m (275 yards) from my camp and 100 metres (110 yards) up a steep slope there was an area of hazel bushes that had recently been thinned . This provided more than enough material for the structures that I was planning. Of course, we had to drag all of it down a very steep and slippery trail to the camp. It worth therefore worth choosing the location of your camp according to how close you are to your building materials, rather than prioritising a beautiful setting. During periods of heavy rainfall, rivers carry wood downstream. Logs can often be found caught at tight curves, getting washed up on the banks and holding up other pieces of wood, branches and logs in their turn. Such spots offer bushcrafters plenty of material for their camps. Forest clearings  also tend to be veritable treasure troves of bushcraft material.

Finding boards for a table, shelf or a shingle roof in the middle of

nowhere is far from easy, and trying to whittle down board-like broken pieces of wood with your pocket knife or splitting wedge is also difficult (, , ). As such, it is best to look for pieces of wood that are already flat and thin. This type of board tends to be most prevalent around broken tree trunks that have been snapped in two under the weight of snow or by strong winds.

You will often see metre-long (about 3 ft) broken shards of wood protruding upwards from the stumps of such trees (**6**, **7**). Another good source of these sorts of boards is rotten old fir tree stumps. These stumps are soft and mouldy on the inside, while the outermost growth rings often remain sturdy, as they contain resin. These stronger parts are often easy to split with wedges **8**.

Bark foliage, leaves, pine brushwood and moss

Bark
The bark that you need to cover a roof can be removed from dead trees. When looking for pieces of bark that will be easy to detach, bushcrafters cast their eyes over dead trees, looking for places where the bar is already peeling away from the trunk. If you look for such spots and carefully try to prise the bark away with your fingers or a slightly bent stick, you will often find that a considerable amount of it comes away **1**.
To make drinking cups or other containers, you will need to use bark that is still flexible **2**, **3**. This works particularly well in spring, with the bark of recently felled trees. I have found the bark of birch, sweet chestnut, willow, ash, maple and spruce trees to be ideal for making such containers.

Foliage

A thick layer of foliage can serve as an insulating layer or a shelter against the rain. It can be found in particularly large quantities in autumn, when it accumulates on the forest floor . See page 34 for instructions for making a leaf rake that will allow you to sweep up and gather masses of leaves.

Leaves

You can also make an effective roof out of large leaves. I am particularly fond of using fern leaves 5 or large butterbur leaves. When the clay on your clay oven is still fresh (see pages 70–3), you could also cover it with a layer of butterbur leaves to ensure that it won't all be washed away if there is a heavy shower of rain.

Pine brushwood

I am always astounded by how long the pine needles stay on fallen or broken trees. The branches of such trees can be put to particularly good use as a roof for a shelter against the rain, sloping if you wish 6.

Moss

Patches of moss can sometimes be torn up directly from the forest floor 7, particularly if the moss has a sturdy structure of its own, rather than being rooted in the ground. It is also easy to remove moss from rocks or tree stumps. Moss makes an ideal material for sealing roofs. That said, tearing up the forest's mossy carpet leaves large scars on the natural surroundings. In order to leave nature intact and to avoid making a mark on the landscape, sealing roofs with foliage is therefore advised instead.

Using your pocket knife

Suitable penknives

Some of the projects in this book, such as the sloping roof, the bench or the bed, require you to use pieces of wood or a minimum diameter in order to ensure their stability. At around 10 cm (4 in) thick, the crossbeams for the sloping roof were the largest of all the diameters specified for the projects set out here. The diameters for the bed, table and bench were no higher than 6 cm (2½ in). In order for you to be able to work with pieces of wood at this diameter or less, I would recommend a Victorinox pocket knife from the 111 mm series or from the 130 mm Delémont collection. Of course, Wenger penknives from the 130 mm Ranger series are also suitable. For the projects in this book I used the Victorinox 'Ranger Grip 79', which yielded excellent results over three months of intensive use.

The nine safety rules

There are clear rules in place when it comes to teaching children to carve with penknives. Adults would also do well to try to stick to these rules, particularly if there are children in the vicinity.

I will always make sure that my knife is sharp before carving.

Sharp knives can be used with greater precision. They grip better and you don't have to use as much force when working with them. Blunt knives are dangerous as you have to exert greater force when using them, and it's easy for the knife to slip. In order to ensure that the cutting edge remains sharp, you shouldn't use it on stone, metal or glass, as this will soon make the blade blunt. Never plunge the blade of your pocket knife into the ground.

I will always make sure I'm sitting down whenever I carve something.

Carving requires your undivided attention. As soon as you stand up, you should close your pocket knife. If you're walking along with an open pocket knife and you slip or stumble, the blade will no longer be under your control and could cause dangerous stab wounds or cuts.

I will always keep enough distance between myself and other people.

To check whether you're far enough away from the next person, stretch out your arms and rotate them once. If you don't touch anyone, you have enough room.

When carving, I will always move the blade away from my body and the hand holding the piece of wood.

Never cut in the direction of your hand or body. This kind of cutting is only for experienced carvers who are very adept at handling penknives.

I will only have one part of the tool open at any one time.

All parts of the pocket knife that are not currently being used are to be folded away, to ensure that you won't be able to hurt yourself on them.

I will always put my knife away once I no longer need it.

An open knife left lying around is dangerous, as you or someone else could hurt themselves on it.

When handing the pocket knife to someone, I will always make sure the blade is closed.

To avoid danger, you should try to make sure that your pocket knife is closed if you're passing it to someone else.

I will not carve or saw trees or other plants.

The bark of a tree is not the place for carving a heart or someone's name. Like a person's skin, the bark of the tree has a protective function. The layer immediately under the bark is also used to transport the nutrients that are required by the tree.

A pocket knife is a tool, not a weapon.

You should never threaten or injure other people or animals with your pocket knife. And your pocket knife isn't a throwing knife, either.

Opening and folding the tools

The Victorinox Ranger Grip 79, which I used for this book, is a one-handed knife. The means that you can open it and close it again with one hand. Of course, you could also use both hands to fold a one-handed knife in and out. However, I will take the time here to explain the exact technique for opening and closing it with one hand. If you can operate your knife with one hand, you will have the other hand free for holding or attaching something else. When building your camp, there are a number of situations in which you may find yourself glad that you have a one-handed knife.

Opening

To open your knife, hold it in your dominant hand. Place the tip of your thumb in the opening loop **1**. You can now open your knife by bringing your thumb up with a semi-circular movement in a clockwise direction **2**, **3**, **4**.

Folding

Hold the knife in your dominant hand and press down on the release button – the Victorinox Cross & Shield on the gripping handle – with your thumb. With the index finger of the same hand, push the blade about 90 degrees towards the casing, so that it rolls along your thumb **5**. Now use your thumb to push the knife the rest of the way into the its bay. At a certain point, the rear spring will take over the closing mechanism, holding the blade in the retracted position.

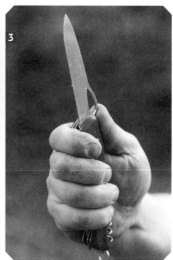

How to hold your knife when carving

If you're carving something, you will need to be sitting down – always abide by this basic rule. Adults can also set a good example by sitting to carve wood, and they'll be looking after their own safety at the same time. Make sure that your seat is sturdy and will not wobble. Place your feet on the ground, a little more than shoulder width apart. Start carving with your legs apart, so that you are working in front of them, or to one side of your legs. Hold the piece of wood firmly towards the back, and support the lower arm of the hand that is holding it against your knee **1**. This will give you a firmer grip on the piece of wood. The hand that is holding the wood should always be behind the knife, never in front of it. Carve towards the ground.

Your tapering movements with the knife have to end in open air. Never support the wood against your thigh and carve towards your lap; major blood vessels run along the inside of your thigh. You should only carve if the wood is in front of your knees.

If there's no obvious place to sit, you could also do your carving kneeling down. As this may mean kneeling on damp or muddy soil, some sort of padding will come in useful. In this position you should make sure that you don't carve against your thigh and maintain a sufficient distance from the nearest person or solid object.

The fist grip

In order to ensure that the force of your arm is effectively transferred to the cutting edge, the knife has to sit firmly in your hand. People often hold their knife too tentatively, so that it is loose within their fist. If you want to be able to carve effectively and safely, you need to grip it so that your hand is firm but not cramped. Don't hold the knife too far down the grip, as this will mean that less of your force will get transferred. If there's just a little bit of the casing sticking out of your fist, you are holding the knife correctly **2**.

The fist grip is the basic grip for working with a pocket knife blade attachment. In order to get a better feel for the carving motion and better leverage, lots of people also place their thumb on the back edge of the knife **3**. Try it out and see what feels best!

The rough cut

The rough cut is a popular basic carving technique, and one that novices should try first. Here you pull the knife away from you through the section of wood to be removed, until the knife comes out of the piece again.

The rough cut can be used to give the piece an initial rough shape or employed if you need to cut a lot of wood away. The long edge of the big blade can produce a lot of wood shavings. By using a rough cut, you are transferring maximum force to the cutting edge. The rough cut isn't suitable for more detailed work, as it's difficult to mete out the force or break off from the carving motion. This type of cut is particularly effective if the cutting edge tilts downwards from the handle and towards the tip of the knife as you move it forward.

Hold the knife in the fist grip. Lay the blade flat so that the handle is as close as possible to the piece of wood. As you push down on the knife and move it away from your body, pull the blade through the wood in such a way that it tilts down from the handle to its tip as you execute the motion **1**, **2**, **3**, **4**.

Exercise: peeling a branch or sharpening the end of a branch: Classic uses for the rough cut include peeling the bark off a branch or sharpening the tip of a branch.

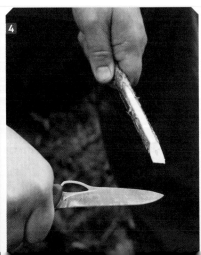

The fine cut

You should also make sure that you are in the correct sitting position when executing a fine cut **1**. For this technique you do not push the blade through the wood using your dominant hand. Instead, the back edge of the knife is pushed forwards through the wood by the thumb of the hand that is holding the piece. This technique allows you to guide the blade safely and with precision, and to stop carving at any point. The fine cut is ideal for carving a groove, for instance. Before executing a fine cut, place the blade of the knife at right angles to the piece of wood and make a cut across, to serve as a breakpoint **2**. To execute the technique, hold the piece of wood a few centimetres behind the area that you wish to carve. Press down on the back of the blade with the thumb of the hand that is holding the wood. The blade will move through the wood without slipping to the side until you reach the breakpoint cut **3**, **4**, **5**. Repeat this process until your groove is deep enough.

Make any boundary cuts first before trying your hand at the fine carving technique if you want to add some decoration or etch a pattern into bark.

Exercise: carving a pattern into bark:

To carve a circular decoration, first cut two round cuts to demarcate the extent of your design into the bark, going right through to the wood itself. These cuts ensure that you won't go outside the limits when you're removing the bark.

Place the blade in the notch that is closest to you and remove the bark up to the frontmost limiting notch. It is important to ensure that you are holding your blade so that it is flat. If the blade is at too steep an angle, the blade will push into the wood. This will require some effort. If you're simply removing the bark from freshly cut wood and holding the knife flat, then you'll find that you don't have to use much force at all.

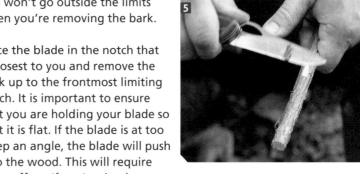

you shouldn't try to tackle any piece of wood with a diameter of over 2 cm (¾ in) or a length of over 20 cm (8 in). Choose a piece of wood that is not too hard and is easy to split, such as hazel, birch, ash or maple.

Using the wood saw

The wood saws found in Victorinox penknives are very sharp. You should always keep the saw attachment closed if you are not using it, for safety reasons. Although your pocket knife saw can be used with both pushing and pulling motions, I would recommend that you stick mainly to a pulling motion. Try to avoid exerting too much pressure on it when you're sawing, instead letting the sharp teeth do the work for you. The rough, interlocking serrated edge makes the saw ideal for moist and freshly cut wood. The trapezoidal cross section of the saw blade allows you to work without too much friction, which prevents the blade from getting stuck. In my experience, these saws remain sharp for a long time.

Aids for fixing the wood in place

In order to prevent any accidents while you're sawing with your pocket knife, you should fix the wood in place so that it doesn't move while you're working on it. You can do this most securely by clamping the piece of wood in a vice or attaching it to a stable base using a fastening clamp. A sawhorse (see page 78) is another reliable tool.

Splitting

If you want to get some dry firewood during wet weather, you will have to split a few branches along their length. Splitting branches is also necessary for a number of projects that involve carving. To split branches, you are advised to use a knife with a fixed blade, rather than a pocket knife. A pocket knife can be used to split branches with a diameter of up to 2.5 cm (1 in). For branches with a larger diameter, you should only drive the knife into the wood until the back edge of the blade has sunk into the wood; at this point you should remove it and continue to split the branch with a wooden wedge. See page 24 for how to make wooden wedges.

To split a branch once it has been cut to length, place it on a firm surface (e.g. a tree stump). The blade is positioned against the cut surface **2**. Using a wooden cudgel, beat the back edge of the knife carefully until it disappears into the wood. Be sure to beat the back of the blade from directly above the wooden surface. Once the back edge of the knife has disappeared into the wood, drive the knife further in by landing careful blows on the front half of the blade **1**. If all goes to plan, the wood will continue to split down its length **3**.

Tip: For your first attempts at splitting a branch or small log,

Fixing wood in place without technical tools

If you don't have a vice or anything similar to hand, make sure that your piece of wood is pressed firmly against a stable surface. This could be a large flat stone, a low wall or a tree stump. If you press it against a ledge or a small hollow, you will also be able to prevent it from sliding horizontally along your surface.

If you secure the piece of wood by clamping down on it with your shoe, you can use your body weight to place a lot of pressure on it, thus avoiding any danger of cutting the hand holding the saw **4**. Your foot will be protected by your shoe **5**.

Boring and piercing with the reamer

This tool is derived from the original knife issued to soldiers in 1891. Back in those days, it was mainly used for repairing the leather straps on the harnesses for their horses. The reamer is very useful in a wide range of situations. It can be used to bore, pierce, scrape, unclog, clean, pre-drill and even sew and works with vastly different materials, including leather, cardboard, plastic, soapstone, aluminium and, of course, wood.

The reamer made by Victorinox has a cutting edge that works in a clockwise direction. It slices into the material, thus acting as a kind of lathe. It also has a hole, allowing you to thread through some string or thread and thus join together suitable materials with a rough seam.

Hold the opened reamer attachment between your thumb and index finger **6**, **7**. This will give you a good level of control over the tool. If you support the reamer with your thumb and index finger, you will feel instantly if the reamer is about to fold up. A note of caution: you could injure yourself if the reamer closes unexpectedly. As such, when working with the reamer you need to give it your complete attention, as you would when using the blades.

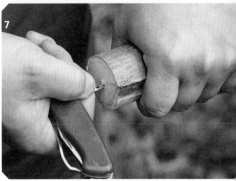

Legal aspects, codes of conduct and the position of your camp

Do you need a permit to create a camp?

The legal situation surrounding wild camping and bivouacking varies from country to country, and there is often a plethora of local regulations and grey areas, which means that we can only set out some general guidelines here. In legal terms, a distinction may also be made between staying overnight in a camp or merely spending the day there. Given that the construction and use of a shelter is equated with camping in a tent, it is possible to give a few rough pointers.

In many countries, each forest plot belongs to an owner. This means that no matter which forest you are visiting, you are there merely as a 'guest'. Despite this, most forests are open to the public and freely accessible, as long as they are not used to excess. To make sure that you're on the right side of the law when building a camp, it is best to obtain the consent of the owner of the area of forest. Check with him or her whether you also need other permits from the forestry service or the local hunting advisory body. That said, in the past I have built small-scale camps without needing to obtain any official permit.

If you know that you're only going to be needing the camp for one night and won't be returning to the area, or that you won't be visiting the camp again for a long time, you are advised to dismantle your camp and remove all traces of your presence there. You should leave the natural surroundings that have played host to you exactly as you found them as a matter of course. In addition, it is worth bearing in mind that if you're not staying in your camp, it will start to rot and eventually collapse, perhaps under a load of snow or in a storm, or possibly also due to children or animals starting using it. As such, you should demolish it to avoid the risk of someone getting hurt.

If you're planning to go the whole hog, like in this book, and build a full-scale camp with a fireplace, table and bench, shelving, hammock, fridge and stone oven, you should definitely heed the applicable guidelines and obtain permission. (For my camp, I obtained an official permit from the local authorities, which can be done without too much effort. To do so, I had to submit an application that was approved on the condition that I would not cut down any green wood on the site to make my camp and that I would only be able to leave the site once my camp had been removed by the forestry service.)

Are you allowed to sleep in the forest overnight?

While wild camping in a tent is forbidden in some countries, other places are more flexible. Specific regulations may apply at a local level. Outside nature reserves and in the absence of any explicit official prohibitions, considerate camping or bivouacking in forest areas may be acceptable, at least when only a small number of people are staying for one night. You should avoid nature reserves, wetland habitats, areas of moorland, water meadows, woodland pastures, young forests, deer crossings or other areas with lots of traces of wildlife (animal dens, tracks or scat), as these areas are habitats frequented by animals. If you want to construct your camp on private property, you are advised to come to an agreement with the landowner first. Whenever possible, walk on existing paths or hardy surfaces like rocks, scree or open, barren stretches of the forest floor. Adapt your camp to your natural surroundings rather than the other way around. Good camping grounds are found, not made!

Leave no trace

People are taking up new hobbies that are practised outdoors in increasing numbers. These pursuits include geocaching, canyoning, kayaking, mountain biking, walking, freeriding, cross-country skiing and survival training.

Traditional pastimes like hiking, climbing, mushroom picking, looking for crystals and gold panning are also undergoing a renaissance and are more popular than ever. However, this trend, while it is to be welcomed in itself, nevertheless poses certain dangers to nature. While practising their hobbies, people venture more frequently and further into vulnerable natural areas. Bushcrafters, too, often find that the ultimate experience is camping in unspoilt natural surroundings, where they are unlikely to see other people. Yet it is precisely these pristine habitats that are becoming increasingly rare, which means that they need to be protected more than ever. It is important to act responsibly and to be aware of the potential effect of outdoor activities on the environment and natural world. The broad 'leave no trace' approach encompasses a number of basic rules that are worth heeding. As there are different regulations in place for each country, district and canton, the following advice is limited to principles that apply everywhere.

Protecting landscapes and plants

Make sure that your behaviour doesn't skew the environmental balance of sensitive habitats for plants and animals. For instance, avoid breaking or sawing branches unnecessarily or carving into bark. Do not pick or disturb plants if you do not need them.

When gathering plants for eating or as a natural remedy, make sure that you do not remove all of the plants of a particular species from one place – always leave a few of them where they are. Protected plants should remain untouched. When you are leaving a spot after having slept or spent some time there, you should try to remove all traces of your presence. Dismantle any shelters or fireplaces, even if they are made of natural materials, and put everything back as you found it, as far as you are able.

Protecting animals

Landscapes that offer a good range of food and shelter but little in the way of disturbances are crucial for wild animals. Observe them only from a distance – do not follow them or feed them. Feeding harms animals, changes their natural behaviour and makes them more vulnerable because they lose their natural timidity. Be particularly considerate around the times when animals are building their nests, breeding, raising their young and in winter. Avoid disturbing them in any way and do not make any changes to animal dwellings. Be quiet, let the noises of nature predominate and keep any dogs under control.

Fires in forests

In most forests, fires are prohibited apart from at publicly established fireplaces. Wherever you are, you should find out about the current risk of forest fires. Avoid lighting fires in strong winds due to the danger of flying sparks. If possible, use existing fireplaces. Never leave the fire unattended and let it burn out completely until only the ashes remain. Always put out fires with lots of water. Smouldering fires can also spread along roots underground. Be aware also that fires leave scars on the forest floor. Gas cookers, gasoline stoves, wood-fired gas cookers, hobo stoves, Esbit stoves, camping stoves and the like are better for warming up dishes than an open fire, as they are safer when used correctly and are less damaging to the natural surroundings.

Leaving no waste

It goes without saying that you should pack up any rubbish and take it home with you. In other words, everything that you have brought into the great outdoors should be gathered up again when you leave. Even more commendable would be to collect and remove any rubbish that others have left behind them. Packaging left over from any provisions is best disposed of at home.

Going to the loo outdoors

The most environmentally friendly way of doing your business in the outdoors is to dig a small hollow, 15–25 cm (6–10 in) deep. Make sure that you go exactly in the hole, burn any toilet paper that you have used and then seal the hole back up again neatly using the loose soil that you have dug up. Stamp on the bit of ground until it is firm again and then mark it with a stick. This ensures that the faeces are sufficiently covered and the next lot of rainfall won't wash it into a stretch of water that you might use for your drinking water. It also prevents animals and insects from coming into contact with the excrement; otherwise flies, for instance, could transfer pathogens to food. The top 25 cm (10 in) of the soil layer contains the microorganisms that are fastest at breaking down excrement; there should be nothing left of it within three days. If the hole is deeper than 25 cm (10 in), it will take little longer for the faeces to be destroyed. You should burn any toilet paper or paper towels within the hollow, or put them in a dog waste bag or an equivalent container and take them home to dispose of there. If it's left on the forest floor, loo paper will take over a year to completely rot away, but burning it speeds up the process considerably. When burning toilet paper you should, of course, be aware of the danger of forest fire. Another option is to use natural toilet paper like moss or large leaves. My favourite is coltsfoot leaves.

Digging a big hole for several people to use over a number of days is not recommended. Larger quantities of faeces break down rather slowly, so the concentration of pathogens and bacteria is high as a result. Having an open hole for several days will also mean that the faeces are completely accessible to flies and other animals. By contrast, urinating in the forest is generally completely harmless to the natural surroundings and people alike.

If several people are spending a few days in the same place, it is worth finding another solution for your toilet. Specialist stores may offer mobile toilets at very little cost.

The biggest risk of transferring pathogens to food comes from negligent handwashing after pooing outdoors. Page 90 shows you how to make an easy mobile handwashing station, plus how to make your own soap.

Choosing the right place for your camp

When choosing the right spot for a camp with a shelter made of natural materials, you will need to weigh up a number of different factors, which have been set out below in order of their priority.

Safety
You should always give the highest priority to your own safety. Be sure to avoid sites that are prone to natural dangers such as floods, falling rocks, landslips, falling trees or breaking branches.

Available construction materials
Another important factor is the amount of resources available in the immediate vicinity such as stones, sand, moss, dead wood, clay, water, binding materials, and so on. In the case of the camp that I built for this book, a farmer had cut back a whole lot of hazel bushes on a steep slope a few months earlier and had left the cut branches lying. Yet despite this find, dragging the wood along a steep forest trail and mud path to the camp, about 100 m (300 ft) below, was an energy-sapping business. It is therefore advisable to set up your camp right beside where you find your building materials.

Surroundings
You will, of course, want to set up your camp in a beautiful location where you will enjoy spending time. However, even the most picturesque spot won't be any good if the natural features present a risk to your camp or there are no or insufficient building materials around. It is best if your camp is a little out of the way and well hidden, so that it won't be chanced upon by anyone wandering around the area. Ideally, it should be protected from the wind and near a source of water. Camping grounds in a dip with permanently damp ground are to be avoided, as are sites in particularly exposed areas or places where there are lots of animal tracks.

Acknowledgements

Lots of people have put a massive amount of dedication and goodwill into the creation of this book. I would like to thank everyone who has contributed towards its success.

Matthew Worden
Quite possibly the best bushcraft photographer of all time! Over these last five months he has not only been my photographer, but also a skilled artisan, trouble-shooter, motivational guru and friend. We have sweated, cursed and laughed together. I still can't repress a smirk when I think about the gross-smelling animal poo in the hollow and our incredible feats of sliding along the steep, slippery path down to our camp in the gorge. Thanks, mate, for all of the hilarious and sometimes exhausting hours, days and weeks that we spent together. I hope that we'll be able to work together again in the future. www.matthewworden.com

My wife, Silvia
Without your willingness to take care of the household and parent Janis almost single-handedly over the months of the project – and all that while pregnant with our daughter, Sarah – it would not have been possible for me to carry out a book project of this magnitude. Thank you for not only accepting my creative outbursts, but actively supporting them. I get the strength and energy that I need to take on such projects from our wonderful family. This book really is a family effort, and it doesn't seem quite right that the author's name is the only one on the cover.

Victorinox
A big thank you to Victorinox. I really appreciate the openness and trust of the company who took me on. I hope that they are happy with this book. I am also grateful for their financial support and the time that I was given to write the book. I am pleased and proud to count myself as one of the Victorinox family!

Andi Thiel
Thank you, Andi, for generously stepping in at the last minute. Just before the deadline, I realised that I urgently needed someone to translate my rustic, Swiss dialect into literary German. I was also looking for someone who would be able to check my technical content when reviewing the text. In you, Andi, I found the perfect combination: someone from the bushcraft and pocket knife enthusiasts' scene who could approach this task both respectfully and instinctively.

Melanie Steingruber
Thank you for letting us borrow your car for a whole month. Doing so meant that we only had to risk the road with the scooter one time (two hefty guys on a 125 ccm motor: we almost came to a standstill on the hills – it was an impossible situation!).

Garage Alder
Many thanks for the wonderful present! Instead of a nice rented saloon to cruise away on a family holiday, we needed an estate for

photo sessions around the camp am to transport what seemed like half the forest around the place … and the Lancia estate was just the kind of Tardis-like vehicle we needed!

Remo Gugolz
Thanks, Remo, old buddy, for your skilled support! The three-legged stool (on page 88) was originally your idea. I hope that our work together will lead to even greater success for the Buchhorn Adventure Garden.

Matthias and Michele Suhner
Thank you for your friendship, your help with building the camp, acting as models for photos and the delicious food. See you in the forest!

Taro
Having a friend like you – someone from the scene who is always up for discussing all things bushcraft (and chatting about other things, of course) – has been hugely valuable for me. Thanks also for your tips on the fridge.

Mike Sommerauer
Huge thanks, my friend, for your tips on 'How to shit in the woods'. I'm already looking forward to our next meeting, sometime, some place.

Abdy Shamloo
Many thanks for your fantastic graphic artwork for the wood-fired gas cooker.

Rubel U. Vetsch and family
I was absolutely delighted to secure the modelling services of the only other self-confessed Rotbach-goer. Thanks, Rubel!

Roman und Karin Brülisauer
Thank you so much, Roman and Karin, for putting your trust in me and letting me set up my camp in your stunning bit of forest in Rotbach.

Markus, Monika and Albert Sutter, their children and Luna
Thank you for believing in me and your wonderful enthusiasm about my book. I'll never forget my first meeting with Albert in the pigsty. He's a great man, although his dog Luna almost ate me alive.

Michael von Büren
Thank you for approving my project proposal so readily.

Pipapi and Grosi
Many thanks for your support and the hat embellishments during the project!

The Holderschwendi clan
Thanks to Regi for the Rotbach tip, to Lars for the photos of Matthew, and to everyone for the brilliant photoshoot!

Roger Kluser and family
Many thanks for agreeing to the spur-of-the-moment photoshoot. It was great to spend the day with you.

About the author

Felix Immler

Born in 1974 in Sankt Gallen, Switzerland, Felix Immler is a social worker who is trained in nature education. He also works as a pocket knife skills instructor at Victorinox. He was one of the brains behind the Buchhorn Adventure Garden in Arbon, on the shores of Lake Constance, and is still active as a project leader there. He specialises in carving, stone grinding, gold panning, knife making, bow making and fire lighting methods. He offers nature experiences and nature education courses and workshops focusing around survival skills and traditional craft techniques.

He is the author of two books on working with penknives, both published by AT Verlag. He offers pocket knife workshops for children and adults in conjunction with Victorinox. See his Swiss website www.taschenmesserbuch.ch for more information and contact details.

VICTORINOX

This book was created in conjunction with Victorinox AG, Ibach, Schwyz, Switzerland.

Note
By its very nature, working with blades, saws and other pocket knife tools entails a certain level of risk. The author of this book has tried, to the best of his knowledge and belief, to set out the safest techniques here and to point out all possible dangers to the reader. The author, the publisher and the company Victorinox cannot guarantee that the techniques described here will be safe for everyone to perform. As such, they assume no responsibility for losses or damages, nor any liability for claims that may be raised in direct or indirect connection with the contents of this book.

Note that for all outdoor activities, the respective regulations relating to the protection of nature, plants and animals apply, as does the weapons legislation in force.

Take a look at Felix Immler's website and YouTube channel:
www.taschenmesserbuch.ch
http://www.youtube.com/user/Taschenmesserbuch

Frances Lincoln Limited
74–77 White Lion Street
London N1 9PF
www.franceslincoln.com

The Swiss Army Knife Book
Copyright © Frances Lincoln
Editor: Asta Machat, Munich / AT Verlag
Photography: Matthew Worden, www.matthewworden.com
Image editing: Vogt-Schild Druck, Derendingen

3rd edition, 2016
© 2015

A catalogue record for this book is available from the British Library.

ISBN 978-0-7112-3889-3

Printed and bound in China.

9 8 7 6 5 4 3 2 1

FRANCES LINCOLN